HIGH SPEED TRAINS TO THE NORTH OF ENGLAND

For my wife Mair, whose support and encouragement
continue to motivate me. Thanks to fellow railway enthusiast
Rick Ward for permission to use his material.

Front cover: Having been refurbished with a new MTU engine yet in unbranded GNER deep blue livery with an orange/red stripe, power car 43290 waits at King's Cross to take her train to the north in June 2007. Carrying the Leeds-London Service advertisement as well as the *MTU fascination of power* nameplate, on this occasion her train is bound for Edinburgh rather than to Leeds.

Back cover: East Coast Main Line 'speedsters' stand side by side at London King's Cross on the evening of 21 January 1980. Deltic number 55 010 *The King's Own Scottish Borderer* has arrived with the 18.11 from York and is joined by IC125 set 254 001, having brought in the 16.15 from Edinburgh, 'The Talisman'.

HIGH SPEED TRAINS TO THE NORTH OF ENGLAND

DAVID MATHER

AN IMPRINT OF PEN & SWORD BOOKS LTD.
YORKSHIRE – PHILADELPHIA

First published in Great Britain in 2023 by
Pen and Sword Transport
An imprint of
Pen & Sword Books Ltd
Yorkshire - Philadelphia

Copyright © David Mather, 2023

ISBN 978 1 39904 265 9

The right of David Mather to be identified as author of this work has been asserted by him in accordance with the Copyright, Designs and Patents Act 1988.

A CIP catalogue record for this book is available from the British Library.

All rights reserved. No part of this book may be reproduced or transmitted in any form or by any means, electronic or mechanical including photocopying, recording or by any information storage and retrieval system, without permission from the Publisher in writing.

Typeset in 11/13 Palatino by SJmagic DESIGN SERVICES, India.

Printed and bound in India by Replika Press Pvt. Ltd.

Pen & Sword Books Ltd incorporates the imprints of Pen & Sword Books Archaeology, Atlas, Aviation, Battleground, Discovery, Family History, History, Maritime, Military, Naval, Politics, Railways, Select, Transport, True Crime, Fiction, Frontline Books, Leo Cooper, Praetorian Press, Seaforth Publishing, Wharncliffe and White Owl.

For a complete list of Pen & Sword titles please contact

PEN & SWORD BOOKS LIMITED
47 Church Street, Barnsley, South Yorkshire, S70 2AS, England
E-mail: enquiries@pen-and-sword.co.uk
Website: www.pen-and-sword.co.uk

or

PEN AND SWORD BOOKS
1950 Lawrence Rd, Havertown, PA 19083, USA
E-mail: Uspen-and-sword@casematepublishers.com
Website: www.penandswordbooks.com

CONTENTS

Chapter One	A Time of Change on the East Coast Route	*6*
Chapter Two	Into Production	*13*
Chapter Three	Into the '90s and Still Going Strong	*50*
Chapter Four	New Millennium. Same Old HSTs?	*68*
Chapter Five	In Final Service, Storage, Withdrawal and Preservation	*125*
Appendix One	Privatisation of the railways and its repercussions in the Yorkshire area	*139*
Appendix Two	Power car liveries	*142*
Appendix Three	Changes in ownership	*143*
Bibliography		*144*

CHAPTER ONE

A TIME OF CHANGE ON THE EAST COAST ROUTE

The year is 1975. The age of the steam hauled passenger train has gone. The age of the diesel express is upon us. Arguably, the route from London to Edinburgh by way of Grantham, Doncaster, York and Newcastle holds a reputation for speed unmatched by any other in the UK. The East Coast Main Line no longer reverberates to the beat of Sir Nigel Gresley's iconic A4s with their instantly recognisable chime whistle. Now it is the thrum of the Class 55 Deltic which fills York station. But nothing lasts forever. There is a new kid on the block …

Since the 1920s the mighty Pacifics designed by Gresley, Thompson and Peppercorn had powered their way between King's Cross and Scotland at the head of such legendary 'flyers' as 'The Aberdonian', 'The Elizabethan', 'The Talisman' and most famous of all 'The Flying Scotsman'. By the early 1960s, their rule was over. The most powerful single unit diesel locomotive in the world had been built on the other side of the Pennines at English Electric's Preston works. After trials to iron out early teething problems, the fleet of twenty-two production Deltics were displacing steam traction and changing the pace of East Coast Main Line (ECML) running forever.

The mighty Deltic locomotives entered service on the ECML in 1961 with the stated objective of hauling expresses between London King's Cross and Scotland to an average speed of 75mph (121km/h), faster than steam power and well within their capabilities. Their two 1,650hp Napier Deltic engines would regularly propel the trains at speeds of 100mph (161km/h) especially as long sections of the route

Racing along the East Coast Main Line and passing Finsbury Park in June 1962 is Gresley A4 number 60017 *Silver Fox*.

Above and left: The world steam speed record holder, ex-LNER Class A4 number 4468 *Mallard* waits at York to take 'Mallard 88', the Settle & Carlisle rail tour, on 17 July 1988. The plaque commemorating the achievement is carried on the locomotive side panels.

York station in Deltic days with 55 011 *The Royal Northumberland Fusiliers* arriving at the then platform 9 heading a King's Cross to Newcastle train on 1 June 1980.

were upgraded for such high-speed running. Originally expected to have a working life of ten years, they would grace the tracks until the end of 1981 when on 31 December the remaining few would finally bow out of regular service.

Electrification of the ECML had been under consideration since the 1930s, but political factors delayed its implementation, with investment instead being focussed on the West Coast route from London Euston to Glasgow which would be largely completed by the mid-1970s, after which work could begin northwards out of King's Cross as far as Hitchin. It would not be until 1984 that the second phase to electrify the route to Edinburgh by way of York would begin. In the meantime, a second fleet of 'stop-gap' express passenger trains would be needed to replace the ageing Deltics and further reduce journey times as line speeds were increased to 125mph (201km/h) over much of the route.

A TIME OF CHANGE ON THE EAST COAST ROUTE • 9

The stage was thus set for the introduction of the InterCity 125s.

The 'Modernisation Plan' which began in the 1950s had at its core a focus on replacing steam traction with the cleaner and less labour-intensive diesel trains. With the opening of the Railway Technical Centre at Derby in the early 1960s this brief was extended to develop new and 'more importantly' faster passenger trains. The ill-fated Advanced Passenger Train (APT) was one such project, with its tilting carriages allowing much faster speeds over existing alignments. A more conventional approach was to lead to the concept of a diesel-electric multiple unit consisting of a Bo-Bo wheel arrangement locomotive at each end of a rake of newly designed carriages. The plan foresaw each loco being powered by a 3,000hp 16-cylinder Paxman Mk3 Ventura diesel engine, this combined power being able to operate a train of ten coaches at speeds of up to 150mph (241km/h). It was envisaged that the trains would normally stay as fixed formations with therefore no requirement to couple and uncouple the locos at terminus stations, thus avoiding light engine movements and facilitating faster turn-round times. The design for the new trains was entrusted to a new Chief Engineer for Traction in 1968. Terry Miller had worked under Sir Nigel Gresley and later as Chief Engineer on BR Eastern Region had

At York on 20 October 1979, Deltic number 55 010 *The King's Own Scottish Borderer* waits to take the 14.11 'stopper' to King's Cross, while the next generation makes an appearance in the background.

overseen the introduction of the Class 55 Deltic fleet. Without major improvements to existing tracks and signalling however, 150mph working was considered unrealistic and a lower maximum speed of 125mph (201km/h) was decided upon. Financial constraints dictated that the new trains would normally be composed of seven rather than ten coaches as originally proposed and to power them the two locos, one at each end, would each need to be able to generate 2,250hp rather than 3,000hp.

But why Paxman? The company founded in 1865 by James Noah Paxman, with Henry and Charles Davey as Davey, Paxman & Davey, Engineers, originally manufactured steam engines, boilers and agricultural machinery. The youngest son of the founder, Edward Paxman, joined the company in 1926 and involved himself heavily in the design of high-speed engines for situations in which space and weight were limiting factors – in short, developing and manufacturing high power to weight ratio engines for use in naval vessels and rail traction. In 1940, the railway locomotive manufacturer Ruston and Hornsby gained a controlling interest in the company, leading to the formation of the Ruston-Paxman Group which became important suppliers of diesel engines for the navy.

As Paxman's engines improved through the 1940s and 1950s, lighter yet more powerful designs were evolved until the Ventura appeared in 1960 and was trialled in the Western Region diesel-hydraulic Warship Class number D830 *Majestic*. After some modifications, the Ventura became a major design used by BR as well as by overseas railways including Germany, Italy and particularly Ceylon (now Sri Lanka). This success led to the development of its successor, the more powerful Valenta. The increased power combined with the novel approach of putting a power car (locomotive) at each end of the train was an immediate success as it delivered the required rail traction without creating excessively high axle loadings which in turn damages the track, especially at high speeds. In 1966, the Ruston-Paxman Group was taken over by English Electric and their diesel engine businesses were merged to form English Electric Diesel Engines Ltd, with Paxman becoming their Paxman Engine Division two years later.

The outline design for the new high speed diesel train emerged from BR's Engineering Department in 1969 following the growing realisation that the APT project would not deliver a fleet of trains until well into the next decade. To counter the growing competition from road transport, a stop-gap was clearly needed. By 1970 and following extensive testing of the new engines, monies were authorised for the construction of an eight-vehicle prototype to be known as the High-Speed Diesel Train (HSDT). The new locomotives would each have a single driving cab, aerodynamic front end and of course a braking system enabling it to run at the increased speeds while still able to bring the train to a stop within existing signal spacing. Passenger comfort would be provided by the latest Mk3 long wheel-base coaches which delivered smooth and quiet travel.

The two prototype locos were built at Crewe Works and numbered 41001 and 41002 while ten prototype Mk3 coaches were constructed at Derby Works. The locos were fitted with conventional buffers, but the coupling gear was hidden behind a removeable screen to enhance the streamlined shape of the set. The horns were positioned above the windscreen while below it were the vehicle's lights behind a second screen, the whole combining to give a smooth, clean appearance. A central single-piece formed the windscreen of armoured glass which protected the driver who sat alone centrally in the cab which had no side windows as it had been claimed that drivers would be mesmerised by distractions at such high speeds, and the only ventilation came from drop-light windows in the cab door. A Pullman version of BR's blue and grey livery was applied in which the two colours were reversed making light grey the main colour.

All previous locomotives had been provided with side-by-side seating for driver and second man, giving both a clear view of the track ahead. The 'single seat' was to prove a major problem area as the drivers' trade union ASLEF was insistent that it needed to be rectified as in their view it paved the way for one-man operation of trains, to which they were strongly opposed. In fact, trade union opposition to the train was to continue for some time in the form of reluctance to work on it without receiving an enhanced rate of pay. Both of these points were at the centre of industrial unrest which resulted in delays in testing the new train. At the rear of the power car was a guard's compartment and a small secondary driving position intended only for low speeds when marshalling trains together. This was a noisy and uncomfortable area for the guard and in later sets was remedied by creating accommodation at the end of a standard class coach. The now largely vacant space this left would prove valuable in later years when it was used to house additional equipment which became necessary as new systems were introduced in response to evolving safety legislation. The prototype, initially based at Neville Hill, commenced running between Leeds,

The prototype HST set number 252 001 on show at Rail 150, the cavalcade at Shildon on 31 August 1975 to celebrate 150 years since the opening of the Stockton & Darlington Railway. From the station, the terminus of the first passenger steam railway in the world, the procession of over thirty icons of the railway age was led by a replica *Locomotion*. The evolution of the railway locomotive passed before our eyes on that glorious Sunday in County Durham, each met with warm applause from the appreciative crowd. An estimated 250,000 people attended the event.

Newcastle and Edinburgh in 1973, often with research vehicles attached in the formation, and on 12 June that year achieved a world speed record for diesel traction of 143.2mph (230.5km/h) between York and Darlington. After about 100,000 miles of test running, the set returned to Derby Works for overhaul, during which the complete set was renumbered to 252 001 and subsequently transferred to the Western Region at Old Oak Common depot for operating over the London-Bristol route where it entered regular passenger service in May 1975, though initially restricted to 100mph (161km/h). It remained in service until summer 1976, only making a reappearance in mid-October of that year to supplement the production sets which were then being introduced.

CHAPTER TWO
INTO PRODUCTION

For the production power cars the front ends would be reshaped and would incorporate a broad single windscreen (following trade-union opposition to the single centrally positioned driver's seat), the absence of buffer gear (though eight locomotives were fitted with front end buffers when conscripted into use as surrogate Driving Van Trailers with Class 91 electric locos for a short time from 1987, which were retained when the eight returned to normal duties) and the warning horns and lights embedded together below the cab windscreen. This was formed of 25mm thick laminated glass designed to be resistant to a high level of impact. Internally, modification to the alternator to provide improved power to the air conditioning, lighting and catering equipment on board the train confirmed the sets as fixed formations as this rendered them incompatible with existing locos and coaching stock. Another problem on the early sets was caused by the disc brakes on the coaches which gave off an unpleasant acrid smell when braking which was drawn into the compartments by the air conditioning system. This was later remedied by a device which closed the air intakes when the train was braking. The HSDT would be known as HST, the D for Diesel having been dropped, and marketed as InterCity 125 (IC125) with silver InterCity 125 lettering and the BR double arrow symbol on the power car body sides. The standard blue and grey livery would be used for the carriages, but the power cars would have a black and yellow scheme applied forward of the guard's van area. This was trialled on just the first three power cars before the black was replaced by blue.

BR decided that the Western Region would be the first to receive the production HSTs into service, with the Bristol route being especially suited to the high-speed characteristics of the units due to its superb alignment, attributable to Brunel and the GWR, providing ample opportunity for them to demonstrate their full potential. To provide for the maintenance of the HST fleet it was necessary to construct specialist IC125 depots at strategic locations within their operational regions. In April 1974, authorisation was given for the first production order of twenty-seven seven-car sets to be built for the London-Bristol/South Wales route of the Western Region (WR), to be known as Class 253 they would be serviced from depots at Old Oak Common (London) and St. Philip's Marsh (Bristol). For the thirty-two eight-car sets ordered for the London-Leeds-York-Newcastle-Edinburgh route of the Eastern and Scottish regions (ER and ScR), known as Class 254, the maintenance would be carried out at Bounds Green (London), Neville Hill (Leeds), Heaton (Newcastle upon Tyne) and Craigentinny (Edinburgh). The first of these sets, numbered 254 001, arrived at Heaton Depot in August 1977 and all thirty-two sets were on stream by early 1979. The ER/ScR sets featured power cars in the number sequence 43056 to 43119 plus two spares, numbers 43122 and 43123. The standard set for the ER would consist of eight trailer coaches, one more than the WR sets, the extra vehicle normally being a restaurant/kitchen car or a trailer buffet second. To help combat overcrowding, some ECML sets were further extended to nine trailer coaches providing seating for over 540 passengers. At this time, the power cars were regarded as vehicles within a multiple unit and therefore the sets were identified as numbers 254 001 to 254 032. For the WR, construction of the production vehicles began in 1975 and the first deliveries came in March 1976. After intensive testing and crew training, passenger services commenced in the summer of that year, though running to existing timings. As more sets were brought into service and initial teething problems rectified, the full IC125 timetable on the WR was in operation by October 1977. It was testimony to the skill of Terry Miller and his team that the problems that had occurred were small in number and quite minor.

   In a major article for the December 1976 issue of *Railway World* magazine under the header 'Silver Jubilee to HST', writer B.K. Cooper describes BR publicity for the Inter-City 125 in which it was boasted that it would change the nature of rail travel and went on to compare the introduction of the new HST with that of the first streamlined steam locomotives some forty years earlier. Suggesting that the departure of *The Silver Jubilee* from King's Cross ranked with the established sights of the capital, he also noted that on the press trip of *The Coronation* there was much excitement as to how much the train might exceed 100mph (161km/h) and whether it would beat the 114mph (184km/h) of *The Coronation Scot* on the previous day. By way of comparison, on a demonstration run arranged by the Western Region between Paddington and Cardiff, he observed that nobody doubted for a moment that the HST would travel at 125mph (201km/h) in the appointed places. He concluded that it is characteristic of the HST that the traveller accepted its speed without comment, being scarcely aware of it due to the train's advanced suspension and the continuously welded rail over which it raced.

Meanwhile in the corresponding issue of *The Railway Magazine*, Douglas Ferry in his article 'Fastest-ever Diesel-Electrics' expressed his surprise at the accelerated schedules introduced for HST services on the Paddington to Bristol and South Wales route in October of that year which involved speed increases to beyond 95mph (153km/h). Observing that he considered it a bold step indeed to go straight to the full high speed sectional times in one move, he went on to note that the new schedules would be amongst the fastest in the world, heralding a new dimension of speed to British Railways.

During the 1970s, BR was still insistent that the APT was the train of the future and that the HST would only operate on the prestigious inter-city routes until the APT could be fully introduced. Financial constraints being as they were, however, it eventually became apparent that no business case could be made for replacing the nearly new HSTs with APTs, particularly on routes such as the ECML where costly electrification would also be required. It was reluctantly accepted that the APT increasingly looked to be only viable on the already electrified West Coast Main Line (WCML), where speed gains from using the tilting trains would also be more significant.

The technical difficulties encountered and largely overcome on the WR meant that this experience could be put to good use when in July 1977 the first IC125s were introduced on the core route of the ECML in the shape of sets featuring power cars numbers 43056 and 43057, with the result that things progressed much more smoothly and by October 1978 enough sets were in traffic for Leeds and Aberdeen to be added to their destinations. By May 1979, delivery of the order for the thirty-two sets numbered 254 001 to 254 032 had been completed and the full IC125 timetable for the ECML could be put into operation. They proved an unqualified commercial success, which meant that many trains were overcrowded at peak times so on occasions locomotive-hauled relief trains had to be provided. In total 197 production power cars were built at Crewe Works, intended to form ninety-five complete HST sets and seven 'spares' for use when repair work was being undertaken. The power cars were originally numbered from 43002 to 43198 and over the ensuing years all but thirty-six carried names at some stage during their main line service, with many having borne two, three or even four different nameplates during that period.

IC125 power car number 43064 carried the name *City of York* between September 1983 and October 1989 and again from March 1991 to February 1998.

Set number 254 005 led by power car 43065 is seen pausing at York with a trial run/driver training train on 24 October 1977.

Their effect was immediate. Passenger numbers on their routes rose significantly especially on the ECML where overcrowding on a number of services had become a serious issue, driving many customers away from the railway and onto the roads, so much so that a further four sets were authorised, although an additional seven had been requested by BR. To go some way towards making up this shortfall, a decision was made by BR in 1981 to transfer two

WR sets to work over the ECML. Such was the continuing demand for HST sets on this route that further transfers would follow, including two from the allocation earmarked for the 'cross country' services authorised for construction in 1978 which came into operation in 1981. These south west-north east inter-regional HST services included trains between Bristol and Leeds, Plymouth and Leeds and Plymouth and Edinburgh. Many enthusiasts mourned the reduction in locomotive-hauled trains over this route, especially the Bromsgrove to Blackwell Lickey Incline section south of Birmingham in Worcestershire where the IC125s made short work of the almost 1 in 38 climb.

By this time, however, the economic climate in the country was changing and a recession was looming, leading to the government becoming less inclined to commit public funds to the railway system. As the 1980s progressed and the recession deepened it became clear that BR's InterCity sector would lose its government subsidy and with demand on the WR also in decline it was decided that the Midland Main Line (MML) from London to Sheffield would offer more potential revenue in spite of its lack of 100mph+ running. Transfers from WR to MML along with others from the south west-north east allocation were therefore carried out, supplied

On the 'racing stretch' of the ECML north of York at Pilmoor, IC125 sets pass at speed as set 254 006 hurries north (towards the camera) led by power car number 43066 while set 254 007 heads south with power car 43069 at the front on 21 May 1978.

by Neville Hill depot, though again the continuing high demand from the ECML resulted in them being quickly absorbed into the ER operating pool.

An on-going challenge and one that should easily have been foreseen was that of maintaining HST sets in their fixed formations. It had long been routine to swap coaches between sets to cover for short term repairs but keeping the power cars with their allotted formations was an altogether more difficult problem leading to ER/ScR breaking cover and abandoning the process as a lost cause, to be followed inevitably by WR in 1984, resulting in the use of set numbers being discontinued. Another consequence of the 'fixed formation' concept arose when naming of the power cars was being considered. A suggestion was that each of the pair be named after famous pairs of people from history such as Samson and Delilah, Hansel and Gretel or Adam and Eve. However, it was soon realised that this could produce some peculiar combinations when a power car needed to be substituted for maintenance. The re-classification of power cars as individual locomotives at each end of the train, to which individual names could be applied, solved the problem. In 1988, the power cars were formally redesignated as Class 43 locomotives. Over the ensuing years and with the APT being finally abandoned as a national project, BR concentrated on maximising the potential of its now major asset. What had been a stopgap had blossomed to become the backbone of the network. Route mileage continued to be expanded and depot efficiency increased resulting in reduced maintenance times and the revenue-earning capacity of the HST fleet proving to be far in excess of expectations over its first decade in service.

Approaching York at Shipton by Beningbrough with a service from Edinburgh to King's Cross in July 1978 is InterCity 125 set 254 001 with power car 43057 in front.

Passing the London Edinburgh Half Way sign north of York in July 1978 is InterCity 125 set 254 018 with her train for Edinburgh, power car 43091 at the front.

Leaving the site of the former station at Shipton by Beningbrough in July 1978, InterCity 125 set number 254 011 brings her train south from Edinburgh with power car 43077 leading.

Approaching York station from the north in July 1978 with a train for King's Cross is InterCity 125 set 254 016 led by power car 43087.

Entering York station from the south in July 1978 is InterCity 125 set 254 018 with 'The Flying Scotsman' service to Edinburgh which included only one booked stop, at Newcastle. Power car 43090 is leading.

Passing through York station in 1978 is IC125 set 254 009

Newcastle Central station seen from the Castle on 8 November 1978 as HST training set 254 008 takes the goods lines.

Winter still held the Vale of York in its grip during February 1979 as set 254 025 led by power car 43104 approaches Chaloner's Whin Junction to the south of York.

HST set 254 003 leaves the ECML from Selby at Chaloner's Whin Junction to join the line from Normanton and Leeds into York during February 1979. The Selby Diversion, which avoided the town with its swing bridge over the River Ouse by means of a direct line from Doncaster to York, was opened in 1983, at which time the junction at Chaloner's Whin became redundant.

INTO PRODUCTION • 23

Having suffered the indignity of being brought to a halt in York station, set 254 012 creates some pollution from power car 43078 heading the Down 'The Flying Scotsman' service to Edinburgh on 10 February 1979.

Power car 43069 at the head of set 254 007 attracts some attention from enthusiasts at York while waiting to continue with a King's Cross to Edinburgh train in early March 1979.

Having crossed the impressive viaduct on the southern approach to Durham station with the magnificent cathedral in the background, InterCity 125 set 254 018 brings in her train from King's Cross to Edinburgh on 13 April 1979 led by power car number 43090.

Passing Shipton by Beningbrough and the Edinburgh 200 Miles sign during August 1979 is set 254 007 led by power car 43069 with an Edinburgh to King's Cross service.

Leaving York behind, IC125 set 254 025 with power car 43104 leading passes the remains of Holgate Junction platform with an Edinburgh to King's Cross train in August 1979.

Passing the sidings at York Yard North, still controlled by semaphore signals, during August 1979 is HST set 254 001 led by power car 43056 with a train for Edinburgh.

Racing past Hitchin on the ECML during December 1979 is set 254 002, featuring power cars 43058 and 43059.

At the buffers under the massive station roof at King's Cross on 10 February 1990, power car 43013 stands alongside Class 91 electric loco number 91008 – the shape of things to come.

Calling at York station on 4 July 1989 is HST set headed by power car 43160 with 43159 on the rear. From May 1987, Leeds Neville Hill depot had been made responsible for the maintenance of some cross country HST services including the Newcastle to Plymouth diagram seen above.

28 • HIGH SPEED TRAINS TO THE NORTH OF ENGLAND

Arriving at York in August 1992, the northbound 'The Aberdonian' is led by power car 43116 *City of Kingston upon Hull*.

Leaving York station for the north on 18 July 1994 is IC125 set led by 43111 with a King's Cross to Edinburgh service.

INTO PRODUCTION • 29

Entering King's Cross station on 15 July 1978 is HST set 254 001 led by power car 43056 with an express from York. An unidentified Deltic and Class 37 wait in the background.

Heading towards York in the summer of 1978, IC125 set 254 002 is passing the Edinburgh 200 Miles sign near Shipton by Beningbrough on the way to King's Cross.

Passing Morpeth, Northumberland with an Up train in 1978 is Inter-City HST set 254 018. A sharp curve just south of the station has unfortunately been the scene of several train crashes and although after the first as long ago as 1877 the building of a 'deviation line' avoiding the curve was recommended, it was never built. Further derailments on the curve occurred in 1969, 1984 and again in 1994. As was the case with the two previous accidents, the train in 1994 was travelling at 80mph (130km/h) in spite of a Health and Safety Executive estimate that trains would overturn on the curve if travelling in excess of 75mph (120km/h). The Morpeth Curve is reputed to be the tightest curve on any British main line and now has a permanent speed restriction of 50mph (80km/h) in place.

Opposite above and below: As speeds increased and approaching trains became quieter, extra vigilance was needed by those who had to cross the tracks, as here on the 'racing stretch' north of York near Shipton by Beningbrough. The sign opposite the red warning to trespassers reads 'High Speed Trains in excess of 100mph pass this point. Take extra care when crossing the line'. At the time of writing (August 2022) families living in the cottages opposite still need to have their wits about them if they are to negotiate four tracks safely, as the children seen below clearly demonstrate.

INTO PRODUCTION • 31

The phasing in of the Class 254 HST sets onto the ECML during the period 1977 to 1979 came at a time when perhaps surprisingly they were considered to have a main-line life expectancy of only ten years, after which the plan was to transfer them to less demanding duties on secondary routes as a result of electrification and the introduction of the APTs. Electrification of the ECML did take place in the period 1988 to 1990 but as mentioned earlier, the APT project for this route had been abandoned so demand for HST services continued, and in fact increased.

It was during the late 1970s and the early 1980s that the IC125s became the dominant express passenger traction encountered on the ECML and at York station their appearance, though increasingly seen as less of a novelty, still attracted interest from the small but dedicated band of enthusiasts who spent their leisure time at the end of the platforms. As power cars and trailer sets came increasingly to be viewed as an interchangeable commodity, in the 1980s it was decided to paint out the set numbers on the power cars and re-classify them as Class 43 locomotives.

So, what had happened to journey times between London King's Cross and Edinburgh Waverley in the period from the dominance of the route by Gresley's A4 Pacifics to the take-over by the IC125s? In steam days, the 392 miles (631km) between the two capital cities would typically take almost seven hours. The Flying Scotsman service would be timed at six hours thirty minutes, giving an average speed over the full journey of 60.3mph (97km/h). When the Deltics took charge, the time for the Down Flying Scotsman was reduced to five hours twenty-seven minutes, an average speed of 72mph (116km/h). After them, the IC125s would be booked to deliver the same service in four hours thirty-five minutes at an impressive average speed of 85.5mph (138km/h), almost two hours quicker than the steam streamliners.

An HST also holds the world speed record for a diesel train carrying passengers. On 27 September 1985, a special press run for the launch of the new Tees-Tyne Pullman service from Newcastle to King's Cross formed of a shortened 2 + 5 set briefly touched 144mph (232km/h) north of York. The world record for the fastest diesel-powered train was also set by an HST, as on 1 November 1987 with a test run for a new type of bogie for use with the Mk4 coaches on the same route, power car 43102 with 43159 on the rear reached a speed of 148mph (238km/h) while descending Stoke Bank.

In *The Railway Magazine* of December 1976, it was noted under the headline 'East Coast Diversion' that legal powers would be sought by BR in the 1977/78 Parliamentary Session to build a fourteen-mile (23km) long double-track diversion to the ECML near Selby, where the existing route lay across the Selby Coalfield, where subsidence from the new coalfield workings and unusual ground conditions would make it impossible to maintain any sort of train service, even at low speed. It was also observed that the swing-bridge over the River Ouse at Selby would present problems for HSTs, whereas the new line would be laid out with the HST in mind.

The line between Doncaster and York via Selby was opened by the North Eastern Railway in 1871 and later became a part of the ECML. Intermediate stations were built at Arksey, Joan Croft Halt, Moss, Balne, Heck, Temple Hirst, Selby, Riccall, Eskrick and Naburn. With the exception of Selby, all were closed in the 1950s and 1960s. In the 1970s, the Labour Government together with the National Coal Board (NCB) and the National Union of Mineworkers (NUM) initiated a programme of increased coal production, the so-called 'Plan for Coal', partly in response to increasing oil prices but also to maximise the income from coal reserves which was intended for sale mainly for electricity generation in the nearby Aire Valley power stations at Ferrybridge, Eggborough and Drax. A major element of the plan was the construction of a large-scale deep underground mining complex based around Selby which became known as the Selby Coalfield, Selby Complex or the Selby 'Superpit'.

As the Selby Coalfield became a reality, the risk to trains due to mining subsidence increased to the extent that a diversionary route for the ECML was considered essential, to be paid for by the NCB. The new line would be laid out with an operational speed of 125mph (201km/h) in readiness for the new high-speed trains, in contrast to the speed restriction of 30mph (48km/h) in force over the swing bridge at Selby and its nearby sinuous curves. Construction began in 1980 and the line was formally opened for inter-city services on 3 October 1983, the first purpose-built section of high-speed railway in the UK. Trains from the south leave the former ECML at Temple Hirst Junction and connect with the former York & North Midland Railway line to Normanton and Leeds at Colton Junction near Church Fenton. The former section from Chaloner's Whin Junction 'south of York' to Selby was closed to passenger services from 24 September 1983 and is part of the York to Selby Cycle Path while a length between Riccall and York now also forms part of the Trans Pennine Trail and National Route 65. It has a scale model of the Solar System along it with each planet at the correct proportional distance from the sun.

The 'Fisherman Bridge'. The former railway bridge over the River Ouse at Naburn is now adorned with a large metal sculpture of a fisherman with his bike and a dog. Entitled 'The Fisher of Dreams', it was erected in 2000 as part of York Council's 'Creative Communities 2000' scheme.

The Selby Coalfield was closed in 2004 following years of decreasing production resulting from technical issues, an overall reduction in the demand for coal for energy generation and the inability to compete with cheap imports. The power stations at Ferrybridge and Eggborough were closed in 2016 and 2018 respectively, while Drax continues to operate fuelled mainly by biomass in the form of wood pellets and 'petcoke', a product derived from oil refining.

INTO PRODUCTION • 35

A unique pairing at Clifton on the northern outskirts of York on 8 July 1979 as IC125 set 254 005 with power car 43064 on the rear leaves the city for Edinburgh while preserved Gresley A4 number 4498 *Sir Nigel Gresley* brings in the returning 'Yorkshire Circular Tour' from Leeds by way of Harrogate.

Inter-City 125 set 254 030 featuring power cars 43114 and 43115 heads north through Grantham station, Lincolnshire on 1 June 1979. Grantham station is between Peterborough to the south and Newark North Gate to the north on the ECML and marks the northern end of the famous section where Sir Nigel Gresley's A4 steam locomotive *Mallard* set the world record for steam traction of 126mph (203km/h) on 3 July 1938.

In *The Railway Magazine* of June 1980, the renowned railway author O.S. Nock in his regular contribution 'Locomotive Practice and Performance' discussed 'HSTs on the East Coast Route' in which he noted that since their introduction two years before, their performance had been hindered by an inordinate number of speed restrictions followed by the tragic accident at Penmanshiel Tunnel, near Grantshouse, between Berwick upon Tweed and Dunbar on 17 March 1979 when part of the tunnel collapsed during improvement works, tragically killing two workmen. It was decided that the ground was too unstable to effect repairs, so the tunnel was sealed, resulting in the need to direct some trains to Edinburgh by way of Carlisle until a new alignment was constructed in a cutting to the west of the hill. Mr. Nock went on to detail a number of more recent journeys during which the HSTs could show their worth, reaching their designated maximum speed on the fast stretches in the Peterborough-Grantham-Newark area and between York and Northallerton. In a contribution in the same magazine some months later, Mr Nock mentioned that he had had calculations done on a micro-computer which supported his stated view that recently logged runs on the ECML indicated that the trains were not yet running on full power and that as time progressed drivers would become more and more familiar with the power car's potential, especially over the more demanding sections such as Stoke Bank.

In the months following the Penmanshiel Tunnel collapse, London to Scotland services were diverted by way of the Tyne Valley line from Newcastle to Carlisle and then continued to Scotland via the WCML. This route would prove invaluable over the years when engineering work north of Newcastle forced diversions by way of Carlisle. Virgin Trains West Coast HSTs also worked out of London Euston on services to the North West including to Manchester, Holyhead and Blackpool North. However, due to the numerous curves on the WCML, these trains were limited to a maximum speed of 110mph (177km/h) on any part of the route. CrossCountry 2+7 sets made light of the climbs over Shap and Beattock summits on Anglo-Scottish workings such as Bournemouth to Edinburgh, routed by way of the WCML and Carstairs. Their timings compared favourably with those of the more usual electrics, especially in damp weather when the benefit of the rear power car driving over drier and cleaner rails becomes noticeable. Diversions necessitated as a result of engineering work have frequently forced IC125s to be routed away from their more direct routes, including seeing them tackle the demanding Settle & Carlisle line, which perhaps naturally they take in their stride.

INTO PRODUCTION • 37

Inter-City 125 set 254 003 featuring power car 43061 is seen leaving Carlisle on 23 March 1979.

In more familiar territory, 43122 and 43095 are seen at Doncaster on 12 May 1980.

Opposite above: HST set 253 034 with power car 43137 taking part in 'Rocket 150' on 25 May 1980. The event at Rainhill, Lancashire to mark the 150th anniversary of the world's first inter-city railway, the Liverpool & Manchester, was organised by BR London Midland Region and took place over the three days of 24-26 May with a Grand Cavalcade on each day. The drive past was led by replicas of *Rocket*, *Sans Pareil* and *Novelty*, followed by locos representing the major railway companies up to the then present day. Included were LNWR 790 *Hardwicke*, GWR 5051 *Drysllwyn Castle*, SR 850 *Lord Nelson*, LNER 4771 *Green Arrow*, 4472 *Flying Scotsman* and 4498 *Sir Nigel Gresley*, LMS 6201 *Princess Elizabeth*, 46229 *Duchess of Hamilton* and BR 92220 *Evening Star*. These in turn were followed by BR diesels from classes 25, 45, 55 and 56, concluding with BR's High Speed Diesel Train and Advanced Passenger Train. All this in celebration of that momentous day in 1830 when George Stephenson's *Rocket* left Edge Hill for Manchester after taking part in the 'Rainhill Trials'.

Opposite below: Leaving Doncaster and its motive power depot behind on 28 March 1981 is Inter-City 125 set 254 008 led by 43070 on a working to London King's Cross.

Below left: Having had its HST set number painted out, power car 43066 leads the Down 'The Flying Scotsman' through York station in February 1981.

Below right: One of the last power cars to be built, 43194, is seen under construction at Crewe Works in the late summer of 1982. This final batch, Lot Number 30968, consisted of power cars 43191 to 43198, ordered on 24 June 1980. Number 43194 entered service in September 1982 and was later named *Royal Signals*, a name she carried from October 1985 to December 1989. From April 1994 she was operated by Angel Trains, then from February 2006 by Porterbrook.

The long distance cross country route from England's south west through the Midlands to the north east suited the combination of power and speed provided in abundance by the 125s and over the years they seldom failed to deliver. Inter-City 125 set led by 43120 at Aller Junction with 1E70, the Saturdays Excepted 15.12 Plymouth to York service on 31 August 1982. Here the Torbay Branch to Paignton and Kingswear diverges from the Great Western Main Line between Newton Abbot and Totnes. Aller Junction signal box was closed in 1987 but its 46-lever frame has been acquired and restored for use at Broadway on the Gloucestershire Warwickshire Steam Railway.

Power car 43180 leads its HST set up the Lickey Incline towards Blackwell, south of Birmingham, on 30 April 1983. This, the steepest adhesion-worked gradient on a British standard gauge main line railway, involves a climb of just over two miles (3.2km) between Bromsgrove and Blackwell on the line between Gloucester and Birmingham at an average gradient of 1 in 37.7 (2.65 per cent). Blackwell station was closed in 1965 and the line itself was electrified overhead in 2018.

HST set led by 43186 at Nuneaton on 5 May 1983. Nuneaton railway station in Warwickshire, formerly known as Trent Valley, was opened by the London & North Western Railway in 1847. Today, as part of the WCML, it handles regular services between London Euston, Crewe, Stafford and the north west as well as cross country trains to Birmingham New Street and Leicester and 'locals' to Leamington Spa and Coventry operated by West Midlands Trains.

Entering York station from the north on 21 April 1984 is HST set led by 43064 *City of York* with a train for King's Cross.

The 15.08 Plymouth to York service led by 43183 approaches Aller Junction, Devon on 24 April 1984.

Cowley Bridge Signal Box Junction near Exeter on 29 May 1985 on the former Bristol & Exeter Railway where it joined the North Devon Railway towards Barnstaple. The HST set is led by 43185, a former GWR power car now owned by ScotRail and stored as a parts donor. The building on the right is the New Inn, formerly the Cowley Bridge Inn, now sadly closed.

INTO PRODUCTION • 43

Leaving Doncaster through Bridge Junction on 27 June 1981 is HST set with 43086 on the rear of an Edinburgh to King's Cross working.

HSTs at Newcastle on 5 May 1982. On the right is 43154 with 43181 on the rear while on the left is a cross country train made up of set 253 056.

Leaving York station for Edinburgh on 5 July 1984 is IC125 set led by 43118.

In the early 1980s, the fleet was given a new identity in keeping with the aim to attract more business travel and was repainted from the Inter-City 125 blue and yellow livery to the attractive InterCity 'Executive' livery of white filled-in logo set on a dark grey base, with coaches in beige and grey accented with a red stripe. From 1987 this livery in turn was modified to the InterCity 'Swallow' scheme in which the yellow warning area on the front of the power cars was confined to the cab roof and the lower part of the nose, while the trailer, i.e. coach, livery was continued over the entire locomotive, giving what many considered to be a more aesthetically pleasing appearance to the set, enhanced by the iconic flying swallow logo. By this time, though they formed only twenty per cent of InterCity's resources for moving people, they ran no less than forty per cent of its train miles and BR was seeking to increase its passenger revenue by a quarter and in so doing lift the HST's percentage of train miles to the fifty-five per cent mark.

INTO PRODUCTION • 45

HSTs at King's Cross. Above, power cars 43050 and 43071 wait at the stops for their next journeys to the north on 19 August 1984 and are joined, below, by sister loco 43045 *The Grammar School Doncaster AD 1350*.

At York station on 27 April 1986, InterCity 125 set led by 43155 *BBC Look North* in InterCity 'Executive' livery waits to take the ECML to the south.

InterCity 125 power car 43107 *City of Derby*, with 43106 on the front, enters York station with the 11.35 from King's Cross as 'Peak' Class 45 number 45 124 departs with a Scarborough to Holyhead service on 14 April 1987.

INTO PRODUCTION • 47

At London King's Cross on 2 October 1987, power car 43055 departs northwards.

Leaving York station in a cloud of exhaust smoke during December 1987, power car number 43077 *County of Nottingham* accelerates away to the south.

Power car 43093 *York Festival '88*, a name it proudly carried from February 1988 to January 1997. The city of York markets itself as 'The City of Festivals', with a major event happening every month, sometimes two or three. Notable examples include the Jorvik Viking Festival, York Literature Festival, Eboracum Roman Festival, York Early Music Festival, York Food and Drink Festival and the York Christmas Festival.

Hertfordshire Rail Tours 'Settle & Carlisle Circular', '125 Special No.1' leaves Hellifield on 30 January 1988 led by 43043 in blue and yellow livery with 43100 sporting InterCity 'Swallow' colours on the rear. The charter ran as 1Z25 from London St. Pancras through Derby, Manchester and Blackburn to Hellifield then on to Settle and finally Carlisle. The return route took it through Haltwhistle to Low Fell to join the ECML to Doncaster, then Sheffield and back to St. Pancras.

Contrasting liveries at King's Cross during June 1989 as power cars 43081 and 43058 wait to take their trains to the north. The set led by 43081 carries the InterCity 'Executive' livery while that of 43058 has been updated to the InterCity 'Swallow' design.

CHAPTER THREE

INTO THE '90s AND STILL GOING STRONG

Electrification of the core of the ECML was completed in time for a delayed summer timetable to begin in July 1991, a consequence of which was the cascading of IC125s to other routes, notably to CrossCountry which had been included in the original route planning but had fallen victim to cutbacks in the early 1980s. However, during 1987 to 1988 a problem occurred with the delivery of Mk4 coaches and Driving Van Trailers (DVTs) which were intended for use with the new Class 91 electric locomotives then being introduced. The DVT is located at the opposite end of the train to the locomotive and from it the train could be driven with a set of similar controls, thereby eliminating the need for the loco to run around its train at a terminus station. Until the new rolling stock became available, it was necessary to conscript existing Mk3 coaches to form the new trains and with them eight Class 43 locos which would act as surrogate DVTs. This of course involved considerable modification to the power cars as well as the reinstating of buffers on a cut-away lower cab front reminiscent of the prototype Class 41 locos, as mentioned earlier. The Class 91s worked with Mk3 stock from 1987 until 1991 between King's Cross and Leeds and though the Class 43 was initially employed to provide power to the coaches only, they were soon enabled to provide traction power as well. This combination of Class 91 electric loco and Class 43 power car gave tremendous acceleration, having a combined available power of over 7,000hp, thereby allowing train speed to be increased rapidly up to the maximum 125mph (201km/h) with ease. When the Mk4 stock was eventually delivered, the eight Class 43s reverted to their standard configuration, though the buffers were retained. The eight power cars involved were numbers 43013 and 43014 which were later to see service with Network Rail's 'New Measurement Train' which entered service in May 2003 and 43065 (later renumbered to 43465), 067 (467), 068 (468), 080 (480), 084 (484) and 123 (423) which became the foundation for Grand Central's King's Cross to Sunderland services after having seen employment with the Virgin Trains fleet working the cross-country route. Here they were replaced by Voyager units and went into storage for several years at Long Marston yard in Warwickshire. They were later bought by Midland Mainline and then by Grand Central in 2007 only to be replaced by Class 180 Zephyr units when the six were then transferred to East Midlands Railway (EMR) stock.

Acting as 'surrogate DVT' to a Class 91 hauled electric service calling at Doncaster on 9 October 1988 is IC125 power car number 43065.

Not to be confined to main line passenger services, by the late 1980s HST sets were in demand from rail charter companies for use on their ever popular 'specials'. Here 43082 with 43107 on the rear passes Ais Gill on the Settle & Carlisle route on 8 April 1989 with train 1Z42, The Blackpool and Settle & Carlisle (125 Special), organised by Hertfordshire Rail Tours. Originating at Birmingham New Street, the tour progressed via Manchester Piccadilly and Preston to Blackpool North, then back through Preston and on to Carlisle by way of the WCML. Returning via the S&C to Settle Junction, it then went on through Blackburn, Bolton and Edgeley Junction to return to Birmingham New Street by way of Stoke on Trent and Derby.

Leaving Appleby station northbound on 6 April 1991 is IC125 power car 43198 with 43193 *Yorkshire Post* leading the Hertfordshire Rail Tours 125 Special No.64 'Hills of the North' from Kidderminster to Carlisle with the return via the S&C.

InterCity 'Swallow' liveried HST set led by 43154 with 43073 on the rear passes Clay Cross, Derbyshire on 28 June 1991. Clay Cross is a former mining town near Chesterfield. Its station fell to the Beeching axe in 1967 and today only a bus service links the town to the nearest station at Chesterfield some six miles distant, while the railway runs under the town without stopping. Chesterfield station is on the Midland Main Line from London St. Pancras to Sheffield which is currently operated by EMR.

Passing Church Fenton signal box where the line from York to Leeds and beyond diverges from that towards Normanton, IC125 set led by power car 43065 takes the former route in May 1992. Note the buffers, a reminder of its time as a surrogate DVT.

Passing Barnetby East signal box on 26 June 1992 is InterCity HST set with 43109 on the rear. Barnetby railway station serves the village of Barnetby-le-Wold in North Lincolnshire, on the former Great Central Doncaster to Grimsby line. Though the signal box and its semaphore signals have now gone, the station still sees services operated by EMR, Northern Trains and Trans Pennine Express as well as regular freight workings to and from the Humber ports.

In the late summer of 1992, power car number 43065 is seen at the head of the 07.10 Edinburgh to Poole service passing Scout Green on the WCML, an area of Shap which was a favourite with photographers in steam days. *Jonathan Allen*

Barnetby East signal box and its semaphores were demolished over the Christmas and New Year period of 2015/16. Above, GBRf 66740 *Sarah* passes with coal empties from Cottam Power Station to Immingham GBRf terminal on 18 December 2015. The same fate befell Wrawby Junction signal box and its impressive array of semaphores to the west of the station, below, as they too were demolished and all replaced by colour lights controlled from York Rail Operating Centre.

More than 230 Valenta engines were supplied for use in the new fleet and so robust were they that in spite of the demanding workload they were able to operate for 20,000 hours between major overhauls, with each power car travelling more than 1,000 miles (1,600km) in the course of an average sixteen hour working day. However, the need to operate IC125s well beyond their expected service life demanded that major components would have to be replaced, including engines and their associated systems. The original Paxman Valenta engines had proved robust and reliable but even with careful and regular maintenance, with millions of punishing miles covered they were approaching the end of their working lives. This, together with an increasing concern over exhaust emissions, would signal the end of the line for them, particularly as time went on and engine failures became more frequent. A new V12 high-speed diesel engine designated the MB190 had been developed by Mirrlees Blackstone, the engine division of Hawker Siddeley, which was more powerful than the Valenta (2,400hp as opposed to 2,250hp) but it was heavier. The increased power was considered important as HST sets were being lengthened by the addition of an eighth carriage. With other necessary modifications, the combined weight of the new installations made the power car 3.8t heavier than with the Valenta, which had further implications for axle-loading and suspension. Trials on the Western Region highlighted numerous problems in spite of the best efforts of the maintenance team at Bristol Bath Road and consequently the MB190 experiment was short-lived.

In 1993, a second possible replacement for the Valenta was offered by Paxman in the shape of its successor, the VP185, the first engine to be designed using CAD (Computer Aided Design) which was itself then trialled over Great Western routes during 1994 and the following year on the ECML, to be extended later to four power cars from the Midland Main Line. Once again serious problems were encountered, this time including catastrophic engine seizures, but of necessity these had to be overcome as more and more Valentas were themselves succumbing to unrepairable failures. Midland Main Line especially were committed to installing the VP185 and converted a substantial part of their fleet at this time. After the initial problems were ironed out, Paxman had another success story on their hands.

Also in the early 1990s the railway was being prepared for privatisation (see Appendix 1) and during 1993 it was decided to split it up with passenger operations being delivered by separate franchises to be known as Train Operating Companies (TOCs) beginning in 1994. All rolling stock was to be owned by three Rolling Stock Leasing Companies (ROSCOs) which would lease their stock to the TOCs. The IC125 fleet was thereby spilt with the stock allocated to Great Western, West Coast and ECML becoming assets of Angel Train Contracts while the CrossCountry and Midland Mainline fleet became assets of Porterbrook Leasing.

An almost immediate effect of this split was to be seen as the visual uniformity of the 'Swallow' livery would soon be consigned to history. First of the new operating franchises to change livery was Great Western which was transferred to a grouping backed by private equity firm 3i and First Bus in February 1996. It was later rebranded as First Great Western (FGW) after First Group bought out the other shareholders. In April of that year, both ECML and Midland Mainline were transferred to their new owners, the former to Bermuda-based shipping company Sea Containers who renamed the company Great North Eastern Railway (GNER) and the latter to coach operator National Express. In 1997, the IC125 operators CrossCountry and West Coast were also transferred into the private sector, in both cases being awarded to Virgin Group, thereby completing the privatisation of BR begun in 1994. By the end of the 1990s, the power car fleet was made up of First Great Western (85), Virgin Trains (57), GNER (21) and Midland Mainline (31).

Passing through Doncaster in 1992, 43062 leads an Edinburgh to King's Cross service.

Waiting at Edinburgh Waverley on 13 February 1993 is power car 43121 *West Yorkshire Metropolitan County*, the name it carried between September 1984 and September 1988, then again from March 1991 until January 1999.

The high Yorkshire Dales can be a bleak place in winter with snow and high winds, as testified by the remains of the snow fences protecting England's highest main line station at Dent on the Settle & Carlisle route, where InterCity HST set led by 43065 runs south on 27 February 1993 with a diverted Edinburgh to Birmingham New Street service.

At Clay Cross, Derbyshire on 17 June 1994 Railfreight liveried Class 60 number 60020 *Great Whernside* is alongside an InterCity HST set featuring 43079 and 43013.

Passing the site of the former South Brent station on the southern edge of Dartmoor in Devon on 24 July 1994 is 43067 in InterCity 'Swallow' livery at the head of 1S35, the Sundays Only 11.55 Penzance to Edinburgh Waverley service. Once a busy junction on the South Devon Railway's main line to Plymouth which became part of the GWR in 1876, the station closed to passengers in 1964 and was largely demolished, though some of the infrastructure can still be seen. The signal box stood on what was the island platform.

Waiting at Doncaster during March 1996 and still in InterCity 'Swallow' livery is IC125 led by power car 43158 *Dartmoor The Pony Express*. CrossCountry Trains.

INTO THE '90s AND STILL GOING STRONG • 61

Approaching York and passing Colton South Junction during the summer of 1996 is HST set led by 43156 with 43153 on the rear.

On 17 July 1996, InterCity set led by 43080 enters the station at Lostwithiel, Cornwall, with train 1V50, the Saturdays Excepted 06.40 Dundee to Penzance 'The Cornishman'. Lostwithiel is a small town at the head of the River Fowey, its station being located 277 miles (446km) from London Paddington via Bristol Temple Meads. It was opened by the Cornwall Railway in 1859 and today, in addition to CrossCountry services between Penzance and Scotland, GWR trains from Paddington towards Plymouth or Penzance also call at the station.

At the head of 1E39, the Saturdays Only 14.08 Newquay to Leeds on 31 August 1996, is InterCity liveried HST power car 43051 at St. Budeaux on the Plymouth side of the Tamar Bridge.

At Venton near Newquay on 8 February 1997 InterCity power car number 43157 *Yorkshire Evening Post* is in charge of 1S85, the 07.25 Saturdays Only Penzance to Aberdeen service.

INTO THE '90s AND STILL GOING STRONG • 63

Recently embellished with the name *The Red Nose*, Virgin CrossCountry power car number 43068 is seen at Plymouth with 1S35, the 09.22 Penzance to Edinburgh service, 'The Cornishman' on 20 March 1997.

At Saltash on the Cornwall side of the Tamar Bridge, 43055 *Sheffield Star* leads 1V38, the Saturdays Only 06.05 Leeds to Newquay 'The Armada', on 31 May 1997.

Attracting attention at Par near St. Austell on the Cornish Main Line on 30 May 1998 is Midland Mainline HST set headed by 43077 with 1V38, the SO 06.05 Leeds City to Newquay service, 'The Armada'.

The Midland Mainline SO service, 1E39, the 14.08 Newquay to Leeds City at the Aller Divergence south of Newton Abbot on the former South Devon Railway on 25 July 1998, with 43049 *Neville Hill* in charge.

Midland Mainline set led by 43064 passes Ashburton Junction on the south-eastern edge of Dartmoor in Devon on 8 August 1998 with 1E39, the Saturdays Only 14.08 Newquay to Leeds. The Ashburton Branch was closed to passengers on 3 November 1958 and to goods on 10 September 1962. The now truncated branch was reopened as the Dart Valley Railway in 1969, was re-named the South Devon Railway in 1991 and runs between Buckfastleigh and Totnes, a distance of seven miles (11 km).

Passing Pugham Farm, Tiverton, Devon on 19 March 1999 is 43008 in Virgin Cross-Country livery with 1S85, the Sundays Excepted 07.20 Plymouth to Aberdeen, 'The Devon Scot'.

Midland Mainline HST set led by 43056 at Dinnaton, Devon, leading 1E39, the Saturdays Only 14.10 service from Newquay to Leeds City, on 29 May 1999.

Virgin Cross-Country HST set featuring 43063 passing Cockwood Harbour, Devon on 1 September 1999 with 1S41, the Saturdays Excepted 14.12 service from Plymouth to Edinburgh.

Still carrying the 'Swallow' of the InterCity livery, power car 43029 leads 1V39, the Saturdays Only 06.44 York to Paignton service, passing Creech St. Michael near Taunton, Somerset on 4 September 1999.

Virgin Cross-Country set led by 43090 at Great Aish, Devon, with 1V49, the Saturdays Excepted 06.39 Dundee to Penzance 'The Cornishman', on 6 September 1999.

CHAPTER FOUR

NEW MILLENNIUM. SAME OLD HSTs?

The completion of the privatisation of British Rail in 1997 and the award of franchises to Train Operating Companies (TOCs) in the first instance on the basis of 'lowest-cost bidder wins' saw the demise of the intercity brand, carried by HSTs as 'InterCity 125' and later 'InterCity' with the 'Swallow' logo, to be replaced over time with the distinctive branding of the

Leaving Parsons Tunnel, Dawlish, South Devon on 1 May 2000, Virgin power car number 43184 is at the head of 1V41, the Sundays Excepted 06.46 Newcastle to Plymouth service.

new companies. By the early years of the 2000s HST services through York were in the hands of the TOCs Great North Eastern Railway (GNER) and Virgin Cross-Country, with occasional appearances from sets operated by Grand Central and, more rarely, EMT (EMT). GNER operated the ECML franchise from April 1996 to December 2007 and after a promising start in which services were improved and journey times shortened, confidence in the company was severely dented following two major accidents, the Hatfield train crash in 2000 and the Selby train crash a year later. Although GNER continued to operate, its financial position became increasingly difficult and its parent company, Sea Containers, a Bermudian transport and container leasing organisation, filed for bankruptcy in 2006. The result was that the Department for Transport announced its intention to strip Sea Containers of its franchise and although GNER continued to operate for a short time, the franchise was awarded to National Express East Coast in December 2007.

At Laira Junction, Plymouth on 21 October 2000, Virgin power car number 43157 heads 1V38, the Sundays Excepted 06.04 Leeds City to Plymouth service.

A Virgin Cross-Country set led by 43104 *City of Edinburgh* arrives at Torre station on the Riviera Line in Torquay, Devon on 28 July 2001 with 1E31, SO 08.15 Paignton to Newcastle Central.

Waiting at London St. Pancras on 2 July 2002 is 43046 *Royal Philharmonic* at the head of a train for Sheffield. As long ago as October 1982, six IC125 sets were transferred to the former Midland Railway main line to work out of St. Pancras to Leicester, Nottingham, Derby and Sheffield. From May 1983, a full HST service was introduced over the route whereupon passenger receipts immediately increased by sixteen per cent as journey times were dramatically reduced and passenger comfort was improved.

Virgin liveried 43161 is in charge of a cross-country service calling at Carlisle during the autumn of 2002.

The times they are a'changing on the former Midland Railway route as witnessed by ex-Virgin power car 43184 with Midland Mainline coaches at Chesterfield on the St. Pancras-Sheffield line on 3 December 2002.

Stafford station on 17 May 2003 sees 43099 on the rear of the last Virgin HST service to Blackpool.

GNER HST set led by 43006 *Kingdom of Fife* at Totnes, Devon, with train 1E34, the Saturdays Only 09.25 Newquay to Newcastle on 7 August 2004.

NEW MILLENNIUM. SAME OLD HSTs? • 73

GNER HST set at Carlisle in 2004. Upgrades to the northernmost sections of the ECML forced services to and from the north of Scotland to be diverted through the Border City and the Tyne Valley Line.

At Carlisle in August 2004, a GNER HST set prepares to leave the station.

Having been refurbished with a new MTU engine (see below) yet in unbranded GNER deep blue livery with an orange/red stripe, power car 43290 waits at King's Cross to take her train to the north during June 2007. Carrying the Leeds-London Service advertisement as well as the *MTU fascination of power* nameplate, her train is bound for Edinburgh on this occasion rather than to Leeds.

National Express East Coast was in difficulties almost from the start, suffering from fuel price rises in a difficult economic climate while at the same time it was widely believed the company had paid too much for the franchise and had thereby overstretched itself. A subsequent series of cost cutting decisions resulted in increasing customer dissatisfaction. By July 2009 it had become apparent that National Express was about to default on its franchise and so the Department for Transport began the procedure to establish a publicly owned company to take over the franchise. This came into effect in November 2009 when a subsidiary of the government's Directly Operated Railways, an 'operator of last resort' owned by the Department for Transport named 'East Coast Mainline' (branded simply as 'East Coast'), took over the franchise. The ECML franchise had effectively been re-nationalised.

East Coast's silver livery was designed with the intention that it could be easily replaced with the branding of whichever TOC took over the franchise in due course, this being the stated aim of the Department for Transport from the outset. Subsequently, from 1 March 2015 the new franchise was awarded to Virgin Trains East Coast (VTEC), a joint venture between Stagecoach (90 per cent) and Virgin Group (10per cent). The performance of the company fell below expectation however and in May 2018 the contract was terminated early by the government whereupon in June of that year VTEC ceased trading and another 'operator of last resort', London North Eastern Railway (LNER), was installed to take over. LNER now (2022) operates long distance inter-city services on the ECML between London King's Cross and Edinburgh Waverley and manages eleven stations including King's Cross and York. It inherited a fleet of IC125s (and IC225s) from VTEC and used these extensively until mid-2019, when they were gradually replaced by the Hitachi Class 800 and Class 801 Azuma sets. The last of the Class 43 IC125 fleet worked their final ECML services on 15 December 2019, after which nine of the fourteen sets were transferred to EMR, one set to CrossCountry and the remainder going into storage.

While all this was happening, the long-distance inter-city cross country route through York linking the south west of England with the north east which includes some of the longest direct rail services in the UK had been in the charge of Virgin Cross-Country since 1997 with some services to Leeds, York and Scarborough also operated by Midland Mainline, a TOC owned by National Express. It ran its trains from the south west and London between April 1996 and November 2007 after which it was taken over by EMT, owned by Stagecoach until 2019 when its tenure came to an end and its services were then operated by EMR. The collapse of Railtrack (the government created group of companies which owned the track and its associated infrastructure including most stations) in 2001 had serious implications for the Virgin Rail Group in that the WCML upgrade upon which its finances depended failed to materialise, resulting in both the Virgin West Coast and the Virgin Cross-Country franchises being suspended in 2002. In 2006, the Department for Transport announced its shortlist for the new cross country franchise and, although Virgin Rail Group was included, the franchise was awarded to Arriva CrossCountry from November 2007. The company is branded as CrossCountry and its services are centred on Birmingham New Street with all its trains calling at or terminating there. It also operates the UK's longest direct passenger train, from Aberdeen to Penzance, a journey of over thirteen hours. CrossCountry inherited ten Class 43 power cars and forty Mk3 carriages from Midland Mainline and Virgin Cross-Country, these being gradually overhauled, fitted with MTU engines (see below) and along with two more hired in from National Express East Coast in 2008 to meet heavy demand on summer Saturdays they are still in operation today as their original franchise 'due to conclude in 2016' was extended first to 2019 and then again to 2023 after the company had successfully extended its services to include trains from Newcastle to Southampton and from Edinburgh to Glasgow.

Meanwhile, the TOC Grand Central has been operating passenger services on the ECML. The Grand Central Railway Company Limited was formed in 2000 to pursue open access opportunities following the privatisation of British Rail. After failing in a bid to run services from Newcastle to Bolton and Manchester in 2003, it was successful in its application to operate between King's Cross and Sunderland (and between King's Cross and Bradford Interchange) in spite of opposition from GNER. Their ECML operation began in December 2007 and a full timetable was introduced in March 2008, though 'mechanical problems' led to regular cancellations. The stock involved was composed of six power cars and eighteen Mk3 carriages purchased from Porterbrook. These were the ones modified during the 1980s for use as surrogate DVTs with the Class 91 electric locos then being introduced on the ECML. They were eventually re-engined before being withdrawn at the end of 2017 and transferred to EMT.

By the early 2000s, the IC125 fleet had been operating its demanding schedule of services for almost thirty years and the original Paxman Valenta engines which had done outstanding work for so long were nearing the end of their serviceable life. Possible replacements had been under trial for some time but so far none had proved up to the task. As time marched on and the engine replacement crises loomed ever larger, First Great Western (FGW) were busy trialling yet another alternative, this time from German manufacturer MTU as a possible improvement over their VP185s. Early indications from the MTU R41 engine were impressive, so much so that FGW later announced that all their power cars would be converted to carry this engine. The conversions would be carried out by Brush Traction, beginning in 2006. At the same time, GNER announced its intention to replace the engines on its IC125 fleet from the still operational Valentas and in a surprise move indicated that the largely unproven MTU R41 was also to be their choice. It was during this period of engine conversion that the GNER power cars were renumbered, with 200 being added to their former number to distinguish them from unconverted examples. In addition to the installation of the MTU engine and its associated Brush cooling system, the GNER locos received an upgraded electronic package which included a new and superior wheel-slip protection system which significantly reduced wheel wear, resulting in a considerable saving in maintenance costs at the time. Bodywork overhauls were also continued at this time and though the parent company that owned GNER ran into financial difficulties, the work being undertaken at Brush Traction continued under the new franchise awarded to National Express East Coast, which began in 2007.

At the same time, a new franchise had been awarded to CrossCountry and they too would convert power cars to the MTU engine during 2008 and 2009. As with the GNER upgrades, 200 was added to their original number. Similarly, the three power cars operated by Network Rail and maintained at Edinburgh Craigentinny would also receive the MTU upgrades. This left only Grand Central to continue with its commitment to the original Paxman Valenta engine. However, as part of an agreement to improve reliability and meet exhaust emission standards which would ensure an extension to their track access rights, it had to be accepted that these would be replaced by the MTU engines in due course, a process which began in 2010 with their last pair of power cars leaving Brush Traction on 1 April 2011. Their re-engined power cars had 400 added to their previous number.

CrossCountry HST set featuring 43384 leaving Chesterfield, Derbyshire in freezing conditions on 2 February 2009. The station on the Midland Main Line hosts services operated by EMR and Northern Trains in addition to the long-distance cross country trains between the south west and Scotland.

Although the MTU R41 has proved itself to be a reliable engine with fewer failures than experienced with previous types, this has been achieved at the price of increased maintenance costs as the years have gone by. At the same time, the VP185 engine still in widespread use has overcome its early issues to be regarded as a very capable engine.

The final runs involving an IC125 power car fitted with the original Paxman Valenta engine took place on 22 December 2010 when number 43123 together with already re-engined classmate number 43468 (previously 43068) hauled two return special trains, the 'Valenta Farewell', between Sunderland and York. Not a bad achievement for an engine which entered service in May 1979 as part of a 'stop gap' fleet and yet lasted for over thirty years and covered millions of miles in service. The loco was renumbered to 43423 when she returned to work with her new MTU engine in April 2011, again proudly carrying her commemorative nameplate. Still 'life in the old dog' yet!

Journey number one of four for the 'Valenta Farewell' on 22 December 2010 as Grand Central power car 43468 (already converted) leads, passing Shipton by Beningbrough on the northern approach to York, with the last Valenta-engined class 43 number 43123 on the rear.

A small crowd of enthusiasts has gathered at York station to bid farewell to 43123 as she waits to depart for Sunderland powered by a Valenta engine for the last time.

The commemorative nameplate carried by 43123 as she waits at York station with the 'Valenta Farewell'

Preparing to leave York for Sunderland on a freezing 22 December evening in 2010 with journey four of four for the 'Valenta Farewell' – the final goodbye to the Paxman Valenta engine, now an hour late due to a signal failure north of the station.

Grand Central power car 43467 leads the way at Colton Junction, York on 30 August 2012 with a King's Cross to Sunderland train, and below, the whole train with 43468 on the rear.

Approaching York on the ECML at Colton Junction, East Coast HST set led by 43320 with a King's Cross to Edinburgh train on 28 September 2012.

Coming up to Colton Junction on the Leeds Slow Line towards York on 1 December 2012 is East Midland Trains (EMT) set led by 43043 with 43081 on the rear of 1Z43, St. Pancras-Kettering-York, 'The St. Nicholas Fayre in York' Christmas special. Though fitted with the new MTU engines, EMT power cars retained their original numbers.

NEW MILLENNIUM. SAME OLD HSTs? • 83

Passing a track maintenance operation at York Holgate on 16 December 2012 is East Coast HST set with power car 43274 on the rear of the train to King's Cross.

Winter has arrived in York as CrossCountry HST passes through Colton Junction with a long-distance train for the south west led by 43304 on 18 January 2013.

84 • HIGH SPEED TRAINS TO THE NORTH OF ENGLAND

On the same day, 18 January 2013, an East Coast set races from York up the ECML for King's Cross led by 43296.

At York station on 31 January 2013 Grand Central HST set led by 43484 *Peter Fox 1942 – 2011 Platform 5* waits with a Sunderland to King's Cross service. Below, the nameplate of 43484.

NEW MILLENNIUM. SAME OLD HSTs? • 85

Peter Fox was for a time a LibDem Councillor for Dore and Totley Ward in the suburbs of Sheffield, South Yorkshire where he was a major voice campaigning for increased recognition of the importance of the railway station of that name. He was also co-founder of Platform 5, a company publishing railway books and magazines.

Rolling in under the impressive station roof at York, Grand Central power car 43 480 is on the rear of a Sunderland to King's Cross service on 7 February 2013.

The driver of Grand Central power car number 43467 waits for the 'right away' from York on 7 February 2013 with his train from Sunderland to King's Cross.

Accelerating along the ECML north of York near Shipton by Beningbrough on 8 June 2013 is East Coast HST set led by 43317 with a King's Cross to Edinburgh service.

As concern mounted about track safety, particularly after the Hatfield rail crash in October 2000, work was begun to prepare ex-Virgin Cross-Country IC125 power cars 43013, 43014 and 43062 'together with two Mk2 and three Mk3 carriages' to form Network Rail's 'New Measurement Train' (NMT) known affectionately as the Flying Banana. The train entered service on 9 May 2003 and has the capability to assess the condition of the track to alert engineers to locations needing attention. The on-board recording systems include high resolution cameras, lasers and gyros which allow the operating team to monitor track condition, gauge, alignment, twist and cant as well as checking for wear or damage to the overhead power lines, all this while travelling at speeds of up to 125mph (201km/h), thereby helping to identify faults before they become a safety issue.

The NMT can check the condition of all the main lines in Great Britain, as well as some of the secondary routes, on a four-weekly cycle. This saves a considerable amount of money by avoiding unnecessary maintenance and being able to predict and prevent faults before they occur. Over the years since 2003, the train has been regularly updated, further power cars and carriages added when necessary and the original Paxman Valenta engines replaced with MTU engines by Brush Traction. Since 2020 the NMT has been maintained and overhauled by Loram UK, a railway maintenance equipment and services provider based at the Railway Technical Centre at Derby.

Network Rail's New Measurement Train, the 'Flying Banana', approaches York at Colton Junction on the ECML on 29 June 2013 led by 43013 with 43014 on the rear. Note the buffers, a reminder of a period spent as a 'surrogate DVT' in the late 1980s.

Leading Network Rail's New Measurement Train through Colton Junction on 15 February 2014 is power car 43062 *John Armitt* heading for York. John Armitt is a Fellow of the Royal Academy of Engineering and of the Institution of Civil Engineers and served as Chief Executive of Network Rail. He was knighted in the 2012 New Year Honours for services to engineering and construction.

Leaving York for Sunderland and passing Shipton by Beningbrough on 23 July 2013 is Grand Central set led by 43467, having retained its DVT buffers, with a train from King's Cross.

NEW MILLENNIUM. SAME OLD HSTs? • 89

Near Copmanthorpe south of York on 31 July 2013, East Coast set led by 43302 heads for King's Cross with her train from Edinburgh.

Approaching York near Colton Junction on 30 November 2013 with UK Railtours 'The St. Nicholas Fayre in York 125 Special', St. Pancras to York and return is East Midland Trains set led by 43066.

Leaving York southbound for King's Cross on 4 May 2014 is East Coast HST set led by 43308 with 43367 *Deltic 50 1955 – 2005* on the rear. Below, the nameplate carried by 43367.

NEW MILLENNIUM. SAME OLD HSTs? • 91

One of the few regular East Midland Trains HST services to travel to York is seen speeding south from the city on 18 March 2014. This is train 1Y84, York to King's Cross led by 43082 *Railway Children – the voice for street children worldwide* with 43058 on the rear.

Almost dwarfed by the majestic station roof at York, Grand Central Sunderland to King's Cross service 1A65 waits at platform 3 on 29 May 2014 with 43465 on the front and 43467 on the rear.

Heading south away from York on 29 July 2014 is 43484 *Peter Fox 1942 – 2011 Platform 5* with 43468 on the rear of 1A61 Sunderland to King's Cross.

Racing north from York and passing 'railway cottages crossing' near Shipton by Beningbrough on 30 September 2014 is train 1N90 King's Cross to Sunderland Grand Central service led by 43467.

NEW MILLENNIUM. SAME OLD HSTs? • 93

East Coast HST set led by 43367 *Deltic 50 1955 – 2005* speeds towards York at Shipton by Beningbrough on 26 October 2014 with 1E09 from Edinburgh to King's Cross.

Accelerating along the 'racing stretch' north of York is East Coast HST set led by 43272 at the head of 1S11 King's Cross to Aberdeen on 26 October 2014.

Just three minutes after the preceding East Coast service to Aberdeen on 26 October 2014 came Grand Central's train to Sunderland, 1N90, from King's Cross led by 43467.

Pausing at York on 17 November 2014 is Grand Central's 43480 sporting 'Movember' moustache logo to publicise a global fundraising campaign in support of mental health, suicide prevention, prostate cancer and testicular cancer charities.

NEW MILLENNIUM. SAME OLD HSTs? • 95

Evening at London King's Cross on 18 November 2014 as East Coast Class 91 number 91 117 waits alongside 43313 which will form train 1N35, the 22.00 service to Newcastle.

Rounding the curve towards Colton Junction on the approach to York is East Coast HST set led by 43300 *Craigentinny* in special '100' livery celebrating 100 years of the Edinburgh depot, hauling train IS37 Plymouth to Edinburgh on 18 December 2014.

96 • HIGH SPEED TRAINS TO THE NORTH OF ENGLAND

On 9 April 2015, a Grand Central set from Sunderland to King's Cross with 43465 on the rear waits under York station's massive iron and glass roof with train 1A61 while at the front end, right, 43468 waits for the green light.

NEW MILLENNIUM. SAME OLD HSTs? • 97

Now in partial Virgin branding as Virgin Trains East Coast (VTEC), power car 43257 is on the rear of 1E03 Edinburgh to King's Cross at York on 14 April 2015.

Speeding south towards York on 24 April 2015 is an HST set in partial Virgin branding led by 43305 at the head of 1E13 Inverness to King's Cross.

Shortly after the Virgin HST above came a Grand Central set as train 1A65 Sunderland to King's Cross led by 43423 *Valenta* 1972 – 2010.

As sheep peacefully graze near Colton Junction on 2 June 2015, Virgin HST set headed by 43316 heads south from York as 1E07 Edinburgh to King's Cross.

NEW MILLENNIUM. SAME OLD HSTs? • 99

Heading into York at Dringhouses on 3 June 2015 is Virgin HST set with 43296 on the rear of 1S22 King's Cross to Edinburgh.

Leaving York behind at Colton on 16 June 2015 is CrossCountry HST set led by 43384 with 43378 on the rear of 1V54 Dundee to Plymouth.

Taking the ECML south from York at Colton Junction on 30 June 2015 is train 1E05 Edinburgh to King's Cross led by 43208 *Lincolnshire Echo*.

In full VTEC livery, HST set led by 43311 (out of shot) with 43312 on the rear of 1S11, the King's Cross to Aberdeen service on 30 June 2015. This was the first fully refurbished HST set to be released into service, making its debut as the 14.00 King's Cross to Aberdeen on 20 June, almost four months after the Virgin franchise started.

Approaching York along the ECML near Colton on 7 July 2015 is VTEC HST set still only partially re-branded with 43277 leading and 43238 on the rear of 1S11 King's Cross to Aberdeen.

Heading into York on 7 July 2015 and approaching Colton Junction is CrossCountry HST set led by 43303 with 43384 on the rear of 1E44 Southampton Central to Newcastle.

Fully branded Virgin HST set led by 43208 *Lincolnshire Echo* passes Shipton by Beningbrough with 1E05 Edinburgh to King's Cross on 17 October 2015.

Waiting at York with 1S16 King's Cross to Inverness on 1 December 2015 is VTEC power car 43302.

NEW MILLENNIUM. SAME OLD HSTs? • 103

It's a misty autumn day at Colton Junction as VTEC HST set led by 43302 approaches York with 1S11 King's Cross to Aberdeen on 31 October 2015, while on the rear, shown below, classmate 43367 *Deltic 50 1955 – 2005* still awaits its full re-brand.

Special livery VTEC power car number 43238 *National Railway Museum 40 Years 1975 – 2015* is on the rear of 1E13 Inverness to King's Cross on 1 December 2015, with nameplate detail shown below.

Special livery VTEC 43238 is joined at York station by Grand Central 43484 on the rear of 1A65 Sunderland to King's Cross on 1 December 2015.

Passing Shipton by Beningbrough on the approach to York on 31 December 2015, VTEC power car 43308 *Highland Chieftain* leads train 1E07 Edinburgh to King's Cross.

A novel combination approaches Colton Junction and York on 10 December 2015 as East Midland Trains power car 43081 leads a rake of VTEC coaches as train 1N83 King's Cross to York. On the rear and shown below is 43076 *In Support of Help for Heroes*.

Engineering work on the nearby ECML necessitated diversions through Sherburn in Elmet and Church Fenton to York during the Spring of 2016. On 10 April 2016, passing the site of the former station at Bolton Percy between York and Leeds, now a small nature reserve managed by the Yorkshire Wildlife Trust, is VTEC HST set led by 43320 with 43309 on the rear of the diverted 1S13 King's Cross to Edinburgh service.

Outshopped in Virgin special livery to celebrate 100 years of the Craigentinny rail depot, Edinburgh is 43300 *Craigentinny*, here at the head of train 1E07 Edinburgh to King's Cross passing Colton Junction 'south of York' on 24 May 2016.

On the rear of Edinburgh to King's Cross train 1E07 is VTEC special livery power car 43274 *Spirit of Sunderland* as it heads south from York on 21 June 2016.

Weekend closures of the ECML north of Newcastle for engineering works require Anglo-Scottish services to be diverted over the Tyne Valley line to Carlisle. On 24 September 2016, VTEC set with 43315 in charge of the 15.05 King's Cross to Edinburgh service passes through Haltwhistle. The signal box is Grade II Listed, as are the station house, footbridge, water tank, water crane and the nearby viaduct over the River South Tyne (the 'Alston Arches') on the former Alston branch. *Jonathan Allen*

NEW MILLENNIUM. SAME OLD HSTs? • 109

Looking south along the ECML from the cab of GBRf 66758 hauling a train of biomass from Tyne Coal Terminal GBRf to Drax Power Station on 23 March 2017 as we are overtaken by an unidentified VTEC HST set hurrying towards York.

This special event held on 23 April 2017, during which the ECML was temporarily closed to allow four trains to run side by side from Tollerton towards York, was staged jointly by Virgin Trains, Network Rail, the National Railway Museum, Hitachi and 'Welcome to Yorkshire'. Its aim was to celebrate speed and style through the ages and the heritage and future of the ECML. Along with VTEC HST set powered by 43238 *National Railway Museum 40 Years 1975 – 2015* with 43290 *MTU Fascination of Power*, the iconic line-up featured preserved Gresley A3 Pacific number 60103 *Flying Scotsman*, Hitachi Azuma Class 800 set 800 101 and VTEC Class 225 set led by DVT number 82 205 in 'Flying Scotsman' livery with 91 105 on the rear. *Rick Ward.*

VTEC HST set led by 43317 hurries towards York with train 1E12 Edinburgh to King's Cross, passing Shipton by Beningbrough on 7 May 2017.

Hurrying north from York on 19 August 2017 with train 1S16 King's Cross to Inverness is VTEC HST set headed by power car 43319 with 43313 on the rear.

Another Saturday of line closure due to engineering work north of Newcastle sees diverted VTEC set led by 43318 pass through Prudhoe, twelve miles (nineteen km) west of Newcastle on the beautiful Tyne Valley line on 23 September 2017 with the 07.04 Edinburgh to King's Cross service. The tall NER signal box is still in use at the full-barrier level crossing manually operated by the signalman, as are the semaphore signals. The iron footbridge is Grade II Listed. *Jonathan Allen*

Train 1N81 from King's Cross to York is led by CrossCountry power car 43301 as it approaches Colton Junction on 18 October 2017.

VTEC HST set led by 43318 approaches York near Colton Junction at the head of 1S11 King's Cross to Aberdeen on 30 January 2018.

On the rear of train 1S11 King's Cross to Aberdeen on 25 April 2018 is special livery VTEC power car 43238 *National Railway Museum 40 Years 1975 – 2015* approaching Colton Junction, south of York.

NEW MILLENNIUM. SAME OLD HSTs? • 113

One of the final VTEC HST sets to be seen in the York area features 43317 with 43257 *Bounds Green* on the rear of 1E07 Edinburgh to King's Cross leaving Colton Junction on 1 June 2018.

A light engine move from Leeds Neville Hill to Craigentinny maintenance depot passes through York station as train 0Z43 on 12 July 2018 with CrossCountry power car 43384 leading LNER power car 43272.

Over twenty years have elapsed since Richard Branson's Virgin Trains entered the privatised rail arena to become a high-profile fixture in the passenger train market place, recently linked with another major transport company, Stagecoach, now departed from the UK rail scene. The bright new image of Virgin Group's scarlet corporate colour and distinctive logo were instantly recognisable as the company leapt into the headlines with promises of significant journey-time savings on the WCML with the introduction of a fleet of 'Pendolino' electric multiple units built by Alstom and Fiat Ferroviaria more than doubling the number of paths per hour in operation. However, partly as a result of a failure by Railtrack to meet its commitments to upgrade the WCML to permit the tilting trains to operate at 140mph (225km/h) without lineside signalling by 2005 and the in-cab technology not being ready in time, Virgin was forced to admit it would be unable to comply with its franchise agreement, which was therefore suspended in July 2002. Railtrack itself collapsed four months later to be replaced by the not-for-profit Network Rail.

More problems resulted in Virgin losing its Cross-Country franchise to Arriva (now part of the Deutsche Bahn Group) in 2007 but the belated Pendelino revolution brought welcome success for the company's re-instated West Coast franchise as passenger numbers soared, and in March 2015 the now famous Virgin branding spread to the ECML when a joint venture with Stagecoach to be known as Virgin Trains East Coast (VTEC) was selected to replace the government's East Coast operation. Again, much was promised in an ambitious programme which included the introduction of the government procured Intercity Express Train (IET) which was branded 'Azuma' by Virgin's marketing team. As with their earlier West Coast plans a great deal depended on the delivery of infrastructure improvements and this time it was Network Rail which failed to deliver with the result that VTEC followed GNER and National Express East Coast into history when on 24 June 2018 it was replaced by LNER, a government-backed 'Operator of Last Resort'.

As if to compound Virgin's woes, the government announced in April 2019 that Stagecoach was to be disqualified from the west coast partnership for failing to guarantee certain liabilities, leaving Virgin in the position of losing its flagship WCML franchise again, which may ultimately signal the end of the group's involvement in rail travel in the UK after it withdrew its application for the franchise to operate its trains from London Euston to Liverpool Lime Street in 2020.

NEW MILLENNIUM. SAME OLD HSTs? • 115

Operator of Last Resort LNER now having taken over the East Coast franchise from Virgin Trains (VTEC) sees power car 43367 *Deltic 50 1955 – 2005* leading train 1E15 Aberdeen to King's Cross away from York at Colton Junction on 28 September 2018.

The very late running 1E05 Edinburgh to King's Cross LNER service approaches York near Shipton by Beningbrough on 11 October 2018 with power car 43312 in charge.

A typical misty November day in the Vale of York as HST set led by 43319 with 43 274 *Spirit of Sunderland* on the rear of 1E15 Aberdeen to King's Cross, now in LNER livery, passes Shipton by Beningbrough on the approach to York on 16 November 2018.

East Midland Trains HST set led by 43048 *T.C.B. Miller MBE* approaches Colton Junction, York on 6 December 2018 with 1N83, a King's Cross to York service.

NEW MILLENNIUM. SAME OLD HSTs? • 117

At the head of train 1Y84 York to King's Cross as it heads south near Colton Junction on 15 December 2018 is LNER power car 43300 *Craigentinny 100, 1914 – 2014*.

Leaving York station on 11 January 2019 on the rear of 1E11 Aberdeen to King's Cross is LNER power car 43257 *Bounds Green*.

118 • HIGH SPEED TRAINS TO THE NORTH OF ENGLAND

LNER power car 43208 *Lincolnshire Echo* is on the rear of 1S16 King's Cross to Inverness at York on 20 March 2019.

Below and opposite: East Midland Trains power car 43083 is in a bay platform at York on 20 March 2019 waiting to form 1Y86 to King's Cross. On the front is 43048 *T.C.B. Miller MBE*, shown below along with the nameplate.

NEW MILLENNIUM. SAME OLD HSTs? • 119

With LMS Jubilee 45596 *Bahamas* having arrived at York with 1Z18, Vintage Trains Dorridge to York 'The White Rose' on 27 July 2019, LNER HST set led by 43239 arrives with 1W96 King's Cross to Inverness.

Passing Shipton by Beningbrough on 3 October 2019 at the head of 1E11 Aberdeen to King's Cross is LNER power car number 43320 with 43312 on the rear. The end of the era of LNER's involvement with the IC125 is imminent. EMR is due to take over redundant LNER HST sets to replace those which are no longer compliant with disability access regulations. A total of nine sets owned by the Rolling Stock Leasing Companies Angel Trains (six) and Porterbrook Leasing (three) will be transferred and the displaced EMR trailers are expected to be sent for scrapping.

In very damp conditions on 20 December 2019, a cheery 'whistle' and a wave from the driver lifted the spirit as The Northumbrian – LNER HST Farewell charity special, day three of four, raced towards York at Shipton by Beningbrough. Train 1Z48, Edinburgh to Leeds is led by 253 003 (43006 later renumbered to 43206 when re-engined) with 43112 (later 43312) on the rear, all outshopped in BR's iconic original 1970s blue/yellow/grey livery. The four-day tour began in Edinburgh and ran north to Aberdeen and Inverness before returning, then heading south to Leeds via York and Doncaster and finally on to London King's Cross. Proceeds were donated to LNER's partner charity 'Campaign Against Living Miserably (CALM)', leading a movement against male suicide.

By late January 2020, the worldwide pandemic of COVID-19 had spread to the UK and as a consequence from March of that year the government introduced measures under emergency powers legislation which resulted in restrictions on both individual movements and public travel. A nationwide lockdown was imposed which continued in force until July, followed by a second four-week 'circuit breaker' lockdown in October and a third in response to a further surge in cases from January 2021 until May of that year when restrictions were finally lifted. The economic disruption was grave, and many businesses failed to make it through. The railways almost ground to a halt, only surviving with financial support from the government under Emergency Powers Agreements, but by the later months of 2021 as restrictions had been eased and the mass vaccination programme seemed to have stabilised the situation, passengers returned and the TOCs could gradually reinstate something approaching their normal timetables.

A brief respite in COVID-19 restrictions allowed a visit to the ECML near Shipton by Beningbrough on 28 November 2020 when ScotRail HST set passed led by 43143 with 43179 (shown below) on the rear of train 566H Doncaster Works Wabtec to Slateford Depot, Edinburgh.

NEW MILLENNIUM. SAME OLD HSTs? • 123

In the autumn sunshine at York on 6 October 2021, CrossCountry HST set led by 43301 waits to depart with 1V54 Edinburgh to Bristol Temple Meads, while on the rear is 43378, shown below departing past Network Rail's impressive new Rail Operating Centre.

At York station on 26 August 2021, a CrossCountry HST set calls with 43378 at the head of 1V54 Edinburgh to Bristol Temple Meads, one of the very few HST diagrams remaining in this area.

CHAPTER FIVE

IN FINAL SERVICE, STORAGE, WITHDRAWAL AND PRESERVATION

The authoritative and well respected *Rail* magazine lamented the imminent demise of the HST on the ECML in its issue of 6 June 2019 under the headline 'Everybody is sad to see them go', going on to observe that they could still do what they were designed to do forty years ago. In an article full of praise for the 'world beater' it went on to say that people love travelling in them and noted that they are currently operating at the most reliable they have ever been. The highly acclaimed railway journalist Roger Ford joined in by suggesting that no train has been so good for so long. The bar had been set.

On 11 December 2020 the last of the Paxman VP185 power cars in passenger service was withdrawn by EMR. Still carrying the blue livery of the former franchise holder East Midland Trains, power cars 43047 and 43049 worked two return journeys between Leeds and Nottingham carrying the headboard 'Last Paxman in Service 1995 – 2020'.

The end of an era came to the Midland Main Line on 15 May 2021 when record breaker 43102, acquired from LNER as 43302, renumbered as it appeared in 1978 and repainted into InterCity livery, led the 20.02 St. Pancras to Leeds complete with headboard, with 43274 on the rear. Now retired, 43102 will take its place at Locomotion, NRM Shildon. For the immediate future, HSTs do still live on in Scotland, the south west and on occasional CrossCountry services, and of course as charter trains.

By the summer of 2022, appearances by IC125 HST passenger sets in the north of England had become an increasingly rare event with CrossCountry being the only TOC still using them on a regular basis, on services between Plymouth and Leeds, Plymouth and Edinburgh and Bristol Temple Meads and Edinburgh, and then limited to one return journey per day.

HST services beyond Edinburgh to Glasgow, Aberdeen and Inverness are still operated on a similar frequency by ScotRail while in the south west of England, Great Western Railway run HST trains between Plymouth, Exeter and Penzance. In addition, Network Rail's 'New Measurement Train' continues to monitor the state of the tracks throughout the country.

The TOC Locomotive Services Limited (LSL) operate HST sets for private charters such as The Midland Pullman and the Staycation Express, this in conjunction with Rail Charter Services. The engineering and construction company Colas and Data Acquisition & Testing Services are both using HST power cars to operate test trains (non-passenger services). The preservation charity the 125 Group, dedicated to the promotion of this iconic brand, have preserved four power cars to date, operating from their base at the Great Central Railway (Nottingham), now renamed to the Nottingham Heritage Railway, and have also been responsible for the restoration to operational condition of the prototype power car number 41001. Established in 1994, the 125 Group now also own a small fleet of Mk3 HST vehicles which they operate on special

LSL's blue Midland Pullman set races along the ECML north of York with train 163L, the Finsbury Park to Whitby via Battersby and return 'The Whitby Jet' on 12 November 2021. Former EMT VP185-engined power cars numbers M43055 and M43046 *Geoff Drury 1930 – 1999* (nearer the camera) feature with ex-GWR Mk3 coaches.

'running days'. Since 2014, Sir Kenneth Grange, designer of the distinctive power car front-end, has served as Honorary President of the Group. The renowned industrial designer is also remembered for such products as the Kodak Instamatic camera, kitchen appliances for Kenwood, Morphy Richards and Bendix and 'street furniture' including parking meters, bus shelters and Royal Mail post-boxes. He was knighted for services to design in the 2013 New Year Honours. Membership of the 125 Group is available to all upon payment of an annual subscription, whereupon members receive a quarterly magazine, *One Two Five,* which keeps them up to date with all matters relating to the HST.

Recreating the lost high-speed luxury train first launched in the 1960s, LSL's blue-liveried set The Midland Pullman was launched in late 2020, its inaugural run being on 12 December from London St. Pancras to Crewe and back. Initially it ran without the yellow cab front panel but with an extra light fitted above the driver's window to meet visibility requirements – the first HST to run without yellow ends, which were painted in later. Since then, it has journeyed throughout England, Wales and Scotland with tours over the country's most scenic routes. The luxury all First Class or Full Dining Seats train includes two kitchen cars in the 2+9 formation from which cooked meals are served to tables laid out with bespoke crockery by staff wearing the full Pullman uniform.

Approaching York on 4 December 2021 with the Jorvik Christmas Pullman, the blue Midland Pullman set is led by M43046 *Geoff Drury 1930 – 1999* with M43055 on the rear of 1Z25, Dundee to York via the S&C.

'The Whitby Jet', Midland Pullman/LSL train 1Z43 from Stevenage to Whitby via Battersby, rounds the curve at York Yard North on 9 March 2022. In charge is Rail Charter Services power car 43059, formerly of EMT and the Staycation Express. Though it was due to reprise the train over the Settle & Carlisle route in the summer of 2022, Rail Charter Services announced in April that the service had been cancelled due to uncertain economic conditions and rising costs. A Rail Charter Services spokesman added that it was hoped to reinstate the train over the scenic S&C line in 2023. Bringing up the rear on this occasion is Blue Pullman liveried M43055, shown below. Other TOCs have also cancelled some services for similar reasons.

'Blue Pullman' set led by M43046 *Geoff Drury 1930 - 1999* arrives at Crewe station on 21 May 2022 with the LSL charter train 138R, the 05.18 Barrow in Furness to Paignton. On the rear, below, is 43049 *Neville Hill* in InterCity Swallow livery.

Rail Charter Services / LSL's The Staycation Express reaches Ais Gill summit on the Settle & Carlisle route on 12 August 2021. Former EMT power cars 43058 and 43059 are in charge of a set of ex-GWR Mk3 coaches outshopped in the new green and grey livery. Running every day except Friday (when the set returns to Crewe for servicing and sanitising), the popular tourist train ran throughout the summer of 2021 between Skipton and Carlisle over this glorious line.

Midland Pullman set led by M43046 *Geoff Drury 1930 – 1999* pauses at York on 30 July 2022 with the LSL/MP charter 1Z40, Dundee to York 'The S&C and Jorvik Pullman'. Having arrived by way of the ECML, its return as 1Z43 would take it over the more testing Settle and Carlisle line.

The nameplate carried by M43046 commemorates Geoff Drury, remembered as being responsible for saving LNER A4 4464 *Bittern* into preservation in 1966 followed two years later by Peppercorn A2 60532 *Blue Peter*. Originally operating out of York depot, both preserved locos were much later given on long term loan to the North Eastern Locomotive Preservation Group and extensive overhauls were undertaken, initially at Darlington. In 2014, the Drury family sold 60532 and she was moved to the LNWR Heritage Centre at Crewe where restoration work continues, along with 4464.

Bringing up the rear of Midland Pullman train 1Z40 on 30 July 2022 at York is power car 43049 *Neville Hill*, outshopped in InterCity 'Swallow' livery.

AND FINALLY:
The status of the operational HST power car fleet as of September 2022 is as follows:

IN SERVICE
A total of 124 power cars are listed as 'in service' and are operated by:

ScotRail. Fifty-three cars: numbers 43003, 012, 015, 021, 026, 028, 031 – 037, 124 – 152 (except 140, seriously accident-damaged and scrapped), 163, 164, 168, 169, 175 – 177, 179, 181 – 183. Leased from Angel Trains, based at Haymarket depot.

Great Western Railway. Thirty-nine cars: numbers 43004, 005, 009, 010, 016, 022, 027, 029, 040 – 042, 063, 088, 091 – 094, 097, 098, 122, 153 – 156, 158, 160 - 162, 170 – 172, 186 – 189, 192, 194, 195, 198. Based at Plymouth Laira depot, includes a small number kept as a source of spares.

CrossCountry. Twelve cars: numbers 43207, 208, 239, 285, 301, 303, 304, 321, 357, 366, 378, 384. MTU-powered, allocated to Laira, maintenance carried out under contract by GWR.

Network Rail. Five cars: numbers 43013, 014, 062, 290, 299. MTU-powered, leased from Porterbrook and used for the NMT. Based at Derby depot.

Locomotive Services Limited. Seven cars: numbers 43046, 047, 049, 055, 058, 059, 083. Former EMR power cars, used on the Midland Pullman and Staycation Express turns. Based at Crewe depot.

Data Acquisition & Testing Services. Four cars: numbers 43052, 054, 066, 076. Operated by the Rail Operations Group.

Colas Rail. Five cars: numbers 43251, 257, 272, 274, 277. Former LNER/EMR power cars, MTU engined, leased from Porterbrook who have awarded the contract for their overhaul to the South Devon Railway at Buckfastleigh. Used for 'Test Train' purposes.

Hanson & Hall. Eight cars: 43296, 308, 423, 465, 467, 468, 480, 484. Former LNER/EMR power cars. 43296 and 308 are spares donors.

IN FINAL SERVICE, STORAGE, WITHDRAWAL AND PRESERVATION • 133

In addition, three power cars are listed as in service on the heritage line, the Colne Valley Railway, Essex: numbers 43071, 073 and 082 while 43056 is in First Group livery at the Gwili Railway near Carmarthen, West Wales. The 125 Group has four cars: numbers 43044, 048, 089 and 159 based at the Great Central Railway, Nottingham.

One of the fleet of four former EMT power cars now used by Colas Rail to haul 'Test Trains' on the network, 43257, is seen in service during 2022. Based at Derby RTC, these sets carry out similar checks as do the Network Rail 'New Measurement Train' though with slightly different equipment on board and at lower speeds. On 30 May 2022 43257 and 43251 were in charge of 146T, the Scarborough to Milford Loop Test Train which was scheduled to run on Mondays from 16 May to 5 December 2022.

ON EXHIBITION

A generous donation from Porterbrook Leasing has allowed Crewe Heritage Centre to obtain a second HST power car, number 43081, as a permanent exhibit in the museum. It was built nearby in 1978 and is officially recognised as the 8,000th loco to be constructed at Crewe Locomotive Works. Currently in EMT livery it arrived at the Heritage Centre on 13 September 2021, forty-five years to the day in 1976 when BR officially introduced the HST into service. It joins sister loco 43018, which is finished in Inter-City 125 livery and is currently undergoing cab restoration to as near 'as built' condition as is possible.

Five power cars are displayed as static exhibits:

43000 owned by the NRM, displayed at NRM Shildon. Prototype HST. Following restoration by the 125 Group, renumbered from its original 41001.
43002 owned by the NRM, displayed at NRM York. Named *The Journey Shrinker*. World speed record holder for diesel traction.
43018 owned by Crewe Heritage Centre.
43081 owned by Crewe Heritage Centre.
43102 owned by the NRM, displayed at NRM Shildon.

Exhibited safely at Crewe Heritage Centre on 21 May 2022 are HST power cars 253 009/43018 restored and repainted into BR blue livery with original headlight cluster re-installed, alongside 43081 in EMT livery (no logo), a working exhibit. Crewe Heritage Centre is a railway museum near to Crewe station, occupying part of the site of the former LMS Crewe Works.

IN STORE:

Hanson & Hall Services Solutions Ltd, providers of storage and disposal facilities for the rail industry, have sixteen power cars in store at Willesden and Eastleigh.

Rolling Stock Leasing Companies, companies that own locomotives and rolling stock which they then hire out to other rail operators, also have a considerable number of power cars held in store. The two major companies are Angel Trains and Porterbrook.

Angel Trains has twenty-nine power cars in store, twenty-five at Ely, two at Neville Hill and one each at Haymarket, Edinburgh and Laira near Plymouth in Devon. In 2021, the German train operator RailAdventure commenced UK operations by purchasing eight power cars from Angel Trains, two of which were then exported to Germany.

Porterbrook has twenty-one in store, thirteen at Long Marston, Warwickshire, seven at Laira and one at Neville Hill, Leeds.

As of November 2021, both Angel Trains and Porterbrook are reputed to be considering sending some of their long-term stored power cars for scrapping, along with an increasing tally of Mk3 coaches. At the same time GB Railfreight have expressed an interest in purchasing a number of redundant train sets for conversion to use in carrying parcels and other mail.

A number of other owners have power cars in store at depots across the country including GWR (four at Laira and one at St. Philip's Marsh, close to Bristol Temple Meads station), the 125 Group (two at Ruddington, south of Nottingham, including the world diesel speed record holder 43159, which was on the rear of 43102 for the record-setting run). 43159 along with 43048 and 43089 were later transferred to the operational fleet at the Midland Railway, Butterley.

LSL has one at each of Neville Hill, Crewe and Eastleigh and ScotRail has one at Haymarket.

In total some ninety-six power cars are currently held in store awaiting repair, disposal or as spares donors. Further details can be found on the 125 Group website at www.125group.org.uk.

SCRAPPED:

The prototype power car number 43001 (originally numbered 41002) was cut up after its successful testing and approval, though sister loco number 41001 was saved into preservation as part of the National Collection at the NRM and eventually restored to operational condition as 43000.

Of the 197 production power cars introduced from 1976, by their fortieth 'birthday' only three had been scrapped, all of which were involved in serious rail accidents and damaged beyond economic repair and all three occurred on the Great Western Main Line. The unfortunate three were:

43173 in the Southall rail crash on 19 September 1997
43011 in the Ladbroke Grove rail crash on 5 October 1999
43019 in the Ufton Nervet rail crash on 6 November 2004

ScotRail power car 43140, severely damaged in the land-slide derailment at Carmont on 12 August 2020, was scrapped in May 2021. Following the report by the Rail Accident Investigation Branch which highlighted shortcomings in the crashworthiness of HST power cars and their Mk3 coaches, calls were made by the Scottish Labour Party, supported by the Trades Union the Transport Salaried Staff Association, that ScotRail withdraw its HST sets.

As the years rolled by, 'time' was called on further members of the now aging class as 43061 and 43075 succumbed during the final months of 2021 followed very quickly by 43053, 070, 079 and 140.

In February 2022, power car 43313 was sent for scrapping after having been used by CrossCountry as a spares donor.

As the summer of 2022 approached, the fate of more members of the class was decided as 43069, 193 and 197 were sent for disposal to Simms Metals in Newport, arriving on 31 May.

But thankfully all is not doom and gloom for the iconic design. GWR has breathed new life into its fleet of HST sets, initially by forming eleven four-carriage formations to be known as 'Castle Class 250' to operate between Cardiff and the south west on local services, following the introduction of Class 800 and 802 IEP units on the Great Western Main Line. The power cars will be named after castles in the region. By the summer of 2020, GWR had increased its fleet to fourteen sets featuring refurbished Mk3 trailer coaches heavily rebuilt at Wabtec's Doncaster plant. It expects to run twelve sets each day across the West of England and has plans to increase its stock by leasing fifteen more coaches and seven class 43 power cars from Angel Trains as well as a further five coaches from Porterbrook to use as spare parts for the 'Castle' fleet, bringing GWR's 'short' HST fleet to a total of thirty-five power cars and sixty-three coaches.

By July of 2022, former LNER class 43 power cars 43290 and 43299 had been brought into service as cover for the three yellow liveried NR New Measurement Train power cars 43013, 014 and

IN FINAL SERVICE, STORAGE, WITHDRAWAL AND PRESERVATION • 137

062 as they became the first members of the class to be fitted with the European Train Control System (ETCS), the in-cab technology being introduced to replace traditional line-side signalling. Upon successful completion of rigorous testing the three upgraded power cars were scheduled to be back in service by the end of 2022.

The 125 Group's plan for the back-conversion of power car 43044 to its original configuration of Paxman Valenta power unit combined with a Marston cooler is proving to be more problematic than envisaged as compatibility issues with the coupling to the alternator has turned out to be an unexpected difficulty. The work is being carried out at Ruddington on the Nottingham Heritage Railway where the power car was renamed to *Edward Paxman* in August 2022, having previously carried the name *Borough of Kettering* between October 1993 and October 2004. The *Edward Paxman* name was previously carried by 43170 between June 1995 and October 2007. Further funding now seems inevitable before the conversion can be completed.

The year 2022 also marked forty years since the introduction of HSTs on the south west to north east route and to mark this CrossCountry has repainted power car 43384 in InterCity

One of the highlights of the Diesel and Mixed Traffic Gala held on the Keighley & Worth Valley Railway from 3 to 6 May 2019 was the visit of prototype HST power car 41001, seen here climbing away from Keighley with the 125 Group's Mk3 coaches. The 125 Group had been custodians of the NRM's prototype since 2011, working from their base on the Great Central Railway (Nottingham) to restore it to operational condition after three decades as a static exhibit. The Group's loan agreement ended in November 2019 when 41001 was returned to the NRM, renumbered to 43000.

'Executive' livery and returned it to its original car and unit numbers of 43184 and 253 051. The work was undertaken at GWR's Plymouth Laira Train & Rolling Stock Maintenance Depot and following a test run from there to Exeter St. David's and return on 5 July the set was spotted on a Plymouth-Edinburgh service on 6 July and again the next day with a Plymouth-Leeds train.

Further changes have seen power cars re-liveried including 43040 adorned with '*Falkland 40*' vinyls and 43047 and 43059 transformed into Midland Pullman blue.

'There's life in the old dog yet . . .'

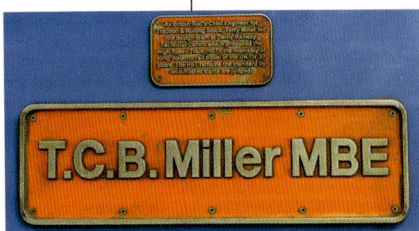 

Above left: The nameplate and plaque carried by power car 43048 in honour of the man who in 1968 was entrusted with designing the IC 125 High Speed Train.

Above right: Edward Paxman is remembered for designing the iconic Valenta engine which powered the IC125s for so long, the nameplate carried here by power car 43170.

Above left: In May 2016 pioneer production power car 43002 was named after the designer of its distinctive nose-cone and interior cab layout. Later acquired by the Railway Museum, York, it is now exhibited on static display in the museum's Great Hall in original Inter-City livery. Prior to preservation, 43002 was owned by Angel Trains and operated by Great Western Railway on its western route out of London Paddington.

Above right: The nameplate carried by power car 43057 to commemorate the depot where the first ECML '254' set featuring 43056 and 43057 was delivered in July 1977.

Right: The nameplate and plaque carried by 43102 which with 43159 set the world record speed achieved by a diesel train. The phrase refers to the description of the train in the Inter-City 125 Review published by BR in March 1978 which went on to describe the HST as the brand-new high speed, high comfort train that opens a new dimension to long distance travellers.

APPENDIX ONE

A BRIEF HISTORY: PRIVATISATION OF THE RAILWAYS AND ITS REPERCUSSIONS IN THE YORKSHIRE AREA

The deregulation and privatisation of the railways was enabled by the Conservative government's Railways Act 1993 which granted powers to the Secretary of State for Transport to transfer separated parts of the railway into the private sector. Passenger services were franchised to TOCs while the national railway-track and signalling company Railtrack sold its track maintenance and renewal operations to private companies to operate under contract to Railtrack. This aspect proved to be a failure as Railtrack collapsed in October 2001 following the Hatfield train crash with all its financial implications. Going into a special state of insolvency for railway companies known as railway administration, it then emerged the following year as Network Rail (same company, new name), described as an 'arm's length' public body of the Department for Transport. Network Rail is now the owner and manager of most of the rail network in Great Britain while TOCs and Freight Operating Companies provide the services.

When the passenger franchises were implemented during 1996/97, a number of franchise holders took responsibility for train services through the Yorkshire area. These included Merseyside Transport Limited (MTL) through its TOC Northern Spirit, National Express (TOC Midland Mainline), Sea Containers (TOC GNER) and the Virgin Rail Group (TOC Virgin Cross-Country).

In 1998, Virgin Group sold a 49 per cent share in Virgin Rail Group to Stagecoach, the Scottish transport group which operates buses, express coaches and tram services in the UK.

In 2000 MTL was purchased by Arriva and consequently Northern Spirit was renamed Arriva Trains Northern. In the same year the first open access operator Hull Trains began running its services between King's Cross and Hull. An open access TOC is one that buys paths on a chosen route owned by a third party for which it takes full commercial risk. Hull Trains was subsequently purchased by First Group in 2003. It was also around this time that the Strategic Rail Authority, the public body set up by the Labour Government to oversee the railway industry, implemented its plans to create a new TransPennine Express franchise, with the effect that from 2004 Arriva Trains Northern's long distance services were transferred to First TransPennine Express while the remainder went to Northern Rail.

In 2007, following the abolition of the Strategic Rail Authority, its functions being absorbed by the Department for Transport and the Office of Rail Regulation, now the Office of Rail and Road, a series of franchise integrations, begun the previous year, saw Virgin Cross-Country taken over by the newly formed CrossCountry while EMT replaced Midland Mainline to operate services out of London St. Pancras. National Express East Coast took over the running of the InterCity East Coast franchise from GNER while in the same year Grand Central began as an open access operator with services between King's Cross and Sunderland.

In 2009, National Express East Coast had its intercity franchise terminated by the government, to be handed to the holding company Directly Operated Railways Ltd a publicly owned company set up by the Department for Transport which would act as the parent company for East Coast. This continued until 2015, when a joint venture between Stagecoach and Virgin trading as Virgin Trains East Coast were awarded the InterCity East Coast franchise.

In 2016, First Group, trading as TransPennine Express, took over that franchise in its own right, having previously been in a joint venture with the multinational transportation company Keolis, while Arriva Rail North commenced operating the Northern franchise.

Virgin Trains East Coast's contract was terminated by the government in 2018 due to 'financial difficulties' to be replaced by the government-owned London North Eastern Railway, an 'Operator of Last Resort' – a business set up to operate a railway franchise if a TOC is no longer able to do so.

In 2019 East Midlands Railway, owned by Abellio, a Dutch transport company, took over the East Midlands franchise from EMT, owned by Stagecoach and then in 2020 the government owned Northern Trains (another Operator of Last Resort) took over operation of the Northern franchise from Arriva Rail North.

In the same year, because the COVID-19 pandemic reduced passenger rail use to near zero, the government took emergency action under Emergency Measures Agreements to support TOCs within the UK by assuming their financial risks, reclassifying them as 'public non-financial corporations', in effect a form of temporary re-nationalisation.

As recently as 25 October 2021, the open access operator Lumo, owned by First Group, began running passenger services on the ECML between King's Cross and Edinburgh, initially with just two trains per day in each direction at off-peak times, increasing to five each way from early 2022, with most taking a little over 4 hours 30 minutes to complete the journey, though no stop at York is included in their schedule. They are operated by a fleet of Class 803 electric multiple units similar to the Azumas in use by LNER.

APPENDIX TWO
POWER CAR LIVERIES

Since the appearance of the prototype HSDT in BR blue and grey livery (though reversed to make light grey the main colour with blue around the window line) the power cars have been outshopped in an array of liveries, from the British Rail blue/yellow/grey which was worn by all, to be followed by variations on the InterCity design ('Executive' and 'Swallow') and then a multitude of distinctive liveries individual to the TOCs operating the HST sets. These included Great Western (green/ivory), GNER (blue/vermilion), Midland Mainline (teal/tangerine) and Virgin Trains (red/dark grey). First Great Western would go on to employ a variety of liveries while Grand Central opted for their striking black and orange colour scheme. National Express East Coast chose what many considered a rather plain white/grey combination while later Virgin East Coast chose a more stylish red and white. EMT preferred the more colourful blue and orange while CrossCountry went for silver and plum.

In more recent times, Great Western Railway have adorned their sets in green, ScotRail have gone for the perhaps more predictable blue and white while EMT have chosen a darker blue. In addition, the distinctive yellow of BR's New Measurement Train and a number of non-standard or advertising liveries have brought further variety to this iconic design. Examples include power cars adorned for the National Railway Museum (43238), First World War commemorative (43172), Queen Elizabeth II Diamond Jubilee (43186) and Queen Elizabeth II 90th birthday (43027). The Staycation Express and the blue Midland Pullman HST sets also now add their distinctive liveries to the well over thirty seen since the sets came into production.

APPENDIX THREE

CHANGES IN OWNERSHIP

Following the breaking up of the British Rail passenger fleet in April 1994 when rolling stock was divided between three ROSCOs ready for privatisation, the IC125 fleet was allocated to two of these dependent upon the route each vehicle worked at that time. These two were Angel Trains, named after the London neighbourhood in which BR's offices were located, and Porterbrook, named after the Porter Brook, a river which passed by the then BR's Sheffield offices next to the railway station. Angel Trains inherited a total of 115 Class 43 locos along with a variety of diesel and electric multiple units (dmus and emus) and over 400 Mk3 coaches, while Porterbrook inherited the remaining eighty-one Class 43s together with a number of Class 47 and Class 73 diesel electric locos, Class 87 and Class 90 electric locos, numerous dmus and emus, almost 650 Mk3 coaches and fifty-two Driving Van Trailers.

Since 1994, several IC125s have changed ownership (some on more than one occasion) either between Angel Trains and Porterbrook or having been sold off by them to smaller ROSCOs created by the Train Operating Companies.

BIBLIOGRAPHY

Cole, Andrew	*Class 43 Locomotives*	Amberley	2016
Coward, Andy	*InterCity 125 – High Speed Tribute*	Morton	2021
Dunn, Pip	*Rail Guide 2022*	Crecy	2022
Llewelyn, Hugh	*InterCity HST 125*	Amberley	2014
Marsden, Colin J.	*HST Silver Jubilee*	Ian Allan	2001
Marsden, Colin J.	*HST: The Second Millennium*	Ian Allan	2010
Morrison, Gavin	*Heyday of the HST*	Ian Allan	2007
Royle, Andrew	*The Train That Saved Britain's Railways*	Crecy	2021
Vaughan, J.A.M.	*The Power of the HSTs*	OPC	1983
125 Group	*125 The Enduring Icon*	125 Group	2018
125 Group	*INTER-CITY 125 Owners' Workshop Manual*	125 Group	2019